Peace through Prayer

REST and RESTORATION for YOUR SOUL

JAMES BANKS

Our Daily Bread
Publishing.

Peace through Prayer: Rest and Restoration for Your Soul
© 2024 by James Banks

All rights reserved.

Requests for permission to quote from this book should be directed to: Permissions Department, Our Daily Bread Publishing, PO Box 3566, Grand Rapids, MI 49501, or contact us by email at permissionsdept@odb.org.

Scripture quotations, unless otherwise indicated, are taken from the Holy Bible, New International Version®, NIV®. Copyright © 1973, 1978, 1984, 2011 by Biblica, Inc.™ Used by permission of Zondervan. All rights reserved worldwide. www.zondervan.com.

   Scripture quotations marked ESV are taken from the ESV® Bible (The Holy Bible, English Standard Version®), copyright © 2001 by Crossway, a publishing ministry of Good News Publishers. Used by permission. All rights reserved.

   Scripture quotations marked MSG are taken from *The Message*, copyright © 1993, 2002, 2018 by Eugene H. Peterson. Used by permission of NavPress. All rights reserved. Represented by Tyndale House Publishers.

   Scripture quotations marked NASB are taken from the New American Standard Bible®, copyright © 1960, 1971, 1977, 1995, 2020 by The Lockman Foundation. Used by permission. All rights reserved. lockman.org.

   Scripture quotations marked NLT are taken from the *Holy Bible*, New Living Translation, copyright © 1996, 2004, 2015 by Tyndale House Foundation. Used by permission of Tyndale House Publishers, Carol Stream, Illinois 60188. All rights reserved.

Interior design by Michael J. Williams

Library of Congress Cataloging-in-Publication Data

Names: Banks, James, 1961- author.
Title: Peace through prayer : rest and restoration for your soul / James Banks.
Description: Grand Rapids, MI : Our Daily Bread Publishing, [2024] | Summary:
   "Jesus offers His children a peace that is gentle and durable. Amid life's
   difficulties, readers learn to unwrap this gift by fostering a daily, heart-to-heart
   relationship with God through prayer"-- Provided by publisher.
Identifiers: LCCN 2023041750 (print) | LCCN 2023041751 (ebook) | ISBN
   9781640702998 (paperback) | ISBN 9781640703001 (epub)
Subjects: LCSH: Peace--Religious aspects--Christianity. | Prayer--Christianity. |
   Prayer--Biblical teaching.
Classification: LCC BV4647.P35 .B35 2024 (print) | LCC BV4647.P35 (ebook) |
   DDC 234/.131--dc23/eng/20231006
LC record available at https://lccn.loc.gov/2023041750
LC ebook record available at https://lccn.loc.gov/2023041751

Printed in the United States of America
24 25 26 27 28 29 30 31 / 9 8 7 6 5 4 3 2

"*Peace through Prayer* is a book I'm going to reread often because there is something in my DNA that causes me to see God as someone to be feared and avoided as much as possible. A woman in an undeveloped country said, on hearing the gospel for the first time, 'I hoped there must be a God like that somewhere.' There is. In a time of high anxiety and fear, this book and the God to whom it refers is the antidote . . . and a refreshing one. Read this book and give it to all your friends."

—**Steve Brown,** founder of Key Life Network, author of *Laughter and Lament*, and radio broadcaster

"True inner peace is one of the rarest things to be found in our restless world. James Banks points the way to a fresh discovery of the supernatural peace God has promised His people."

—**Jim Cymbala,** senior pastor of The Brooklyn Tabernacle

"If you are like me, your heart longs for a conversational intimacy with God, to feel as though He is right there with you every moment, awake and asleep. This book helped me in surprising ways and I believe it can help you. James has such a conversational intimacy with the Scriptures that they pour out of every paragraph. This book might cause you to take your phone and your watch and put them out of sight, so that you can just *be* with God. A must-read!"

—**Robby Dilmore,** The Christian Car Guy broadcaster and retreat leader

"Occasionally I will read a book and think, *I want to read this again. Peace through Prayer* is one of those. In his newest book, James Banks combines rich biblical teaching about prayer with encouraging examples from his own life and from church history. The result is practical help for a more enjoyable and fruitful prayer life. Highly recommended!"

—**David Beaty**, pastor of River Oaks Community Church and author of *An All-Surpassing Fellowship* and *Keep Your Spiritual Edge*

"Reading *Peace through Prayer* feels like receiving an encircling hug from a safe and caring pastor—one who shares with you the life-changing, unconditional love of Jesus. Profound but accessible, this exploration into the gift of peace is one I recommend wholeheartedly."

—**Amy Boucher Pye**, retreat leader, spiritual director, and author of *Transforming Love*

"*Peace through Prayer* is an encouraging and challenging book where James Banks takes stories from Scripture, stories from life, and the truth of Jesus and weaves them all together to point us to a peace that transcends understanding. James gives us practical ideas on how to incorporate prayer into our lives and allow God to lead us every day. This book is great for anyone who is looking to deepen their faith and trust in Jesus and learn how to lean on Him."

—**Chris Sasser**, pastor and author of *Bags: Helping Your Kids Lighten the Load*

To Stefani, Geoffrey, Sarah, Austin,
Leilani, and any who will follow:

"May God give you more and more mercy,
peace, and love."
Jude 2 NLT

Contents

	Introduction	9
1.	Heart First	11
2.	Peace with Our Past: *Changed by Love*	27
3.	Peace We Were Meant For: *Running Home*	43
4.	Peace in Our Worries: *Casting Cares*	61
5.	Peace and Rest: *Carried by God*	79
6.	Peace in Low Places: *Choosing Humility*	93
7.	Hungering for Peace: *Prayer from God's Word*	111
8.	Fighting for Peace: *Armored for Prayer*	131
9.	Pressing through to Peace: *Passionate, Persevering Prayer*	151
10.	The Friend Who Is Peace Forever	171
	Acknowledgments	187
	Notes	189

Introduction

Jesus said, "Come to me, all of you who are weary and carry heavy burdens, and I will give you rest" (Matthew 11:28 NLT). When we think about what those words promise and who is actually saying them, they become some of the most welcoming words ever spoken. In a world that is unraveling with anxiety and stress, no one less than Jesus offers us His peace.

The peace Jesus offers us is more than just words. It's healing for our hurts and calm for our troubled hearts. It's love and acceptance when others misunderstand us and push us away. It's the freedom of a new identity in Him, defined not by how good we are but by how good He is.

The peace that Jesus gives is a lasting peace. After He promised peace to His followers in John 14:27, He immediately added, "I do not give to you as the world gives." He offers us a peace that the world can't touch or take away, even when our lives are difficult. Still, we may sometimes wonder, If Jesus offers me His peace, why don't I have more of it? The simple answer is that Jesus's peace is not automatic. If someone gives us a gift, we have to put out our hands to receive it. If our hands are busy and filled with other things, we won't be able to hold what we're offered.

This book is about opening our hands and our hearts to

receive the gift God wants to give us. In it, we'll look at the promises He makes in His Word about His perfect peace. We'll consider practical things we can do each day to receive His peace, especially through the ways we pray. But this isn't a book about five easy steps or methods; while we have to receive Jesus's peace, it's not something we *make* happen if we say the right words or do things just so. God's peace is far more personal than that; it happens through the warmth and love of a relationship with Him, a heart-to-heart interaction that is enjoyed each day through prayer.

Jesus means what He says. The peace He offers us really is possible. It's there for the asking, and in the asking, we are blessed. Because when we ask, we meet Him. And in His loving hands we find everything we need.

CHAPTER ONE

Heart First

*The best and most beautiful things in the world cannot
be seen nor even touched, but just felt in the heart.*

Helen Keller

The horn was loud enough to wake the dead. At least it jolted me awake.

Moments earlier I had pulled into a hotel entry circle when another driver cut in front of me, clearly in a rush. When the car in front of him took too long to let a passenger out, he signaled his displeasure with a long and emphatic blast. The sound reverberated off asphalt and concrete and turned heads for half a block.

And then I saw his bumper sticker: "Create Peace."

I couldn't help smiling. There's a reason I don't put bumper stickers like that on my car. Too many times I've overreacted or been in too big of a rush behind the wheel in spite of my best efforts to "create peace" in my own heart and life.

Peace can be hard to come by in our never-put-down-your-phone, fit-it-all-in, hooked-on-caffeine-and-social-media world. It seems like anxiety is everywhere, even though technology was supposed to make our lives so much easier. Way back in 1930, the British economist John Maynard Keynes wrote an essay predicting that within a century, technology would make our lives so much easier that we'd only work if we wanted to—at most, just a three-hour workday and a fifteen-hour week.[1] But Keynes missed something important. The faster we go and the easier technology makes our lives in one area, the more we want in another. The human heart is restless—or as John Calvin put it, a perpetual "factory of idols."[2] The void within pulls us in on ourselves like a black hole, yet all the while we're often not aware of it. When our hearts almost automatically careen from one elusive source of satisfaction to another, it's enough to make you wonder if peace within is available to us.

The "perfect peace" God promises in Isaiah 26:3 can find its way in regardless of life's difficulties. This is the experience of God's people throughout Scripture; peace is a gift our Abba Father longs to give to us. It's available to the single mom who's doing her best to put food on the table and somehow have enough energy left to help her little boy with his homework. It's there for the man who thinks he has his whole life in front of him until he receives the pathology report showing a life-threatening battle with cancer ahead. It's accessible to all of us. The Bible points to this peace as something that transforms us, a nearness to the One whose "love is better than life" (Psalm 63:3) because "the LORD is peace" (Judges 6:24 NLT).

The peace God offers to us looks at the future and is not fearful, looks at the past and is reconciled, and looks at the present and is restful. It can do all of this because of the One who gives it, the One who does "all things well"

(Mark 7:37 ESV). Our part is to receive it and walk in it—but that's not always as easy as it seems. I'm reminded of something a wise friend and mentor in ministry told me once during a candid conversation over coffee: "James, sometimes you sound holier than you really are." I winced at the words, but I had to admit he had a point. He was warning me against a faith where we say what we're expected to say but where words that are good and true lose their meaning from overuse and end up sounding like jargon. It's one thing to talk (or to write) about peace; it's another entirely to live there.

And that brings us to some winsome words from Jesus.

Jesus Promised Peace

Jesus told His followers, "Peace I leave with you; my peace I give you" (John 14:27). You can't come away from those words without the distinct impression that He is offering something life-changing and wonderful. Jesus wasn't just saying nice words to make us feel better. He's describing something that's both gentle and durable, something our hearts have always longed for. And He says it so simply and beautifully that we immediately wonder, Have I been making this too hard?

"*My* peace I give you." The peace Jesus offers is His personal peace. It's a peace that's heaven-sent, but like Jesus it's practical and down-to-earth. He isn't describing some ethereal or mystical concept we could only arrive at through years of effort and contemplation. This is a peace that doesn't come from us, but it's within reach. "My peace I *give* you." It's not something we manufacture or make happen. It comes from Him, and He can be trusted. And so He adds, "I do not give to you as the world gives"

(v. 27). Jesus wouldn't make a promise He didn't intend to keep. This is a lasting peace. It's almost palpable as soon as He says the words: this peace is both real and practical, permeating deeper than our fears and uncertainties and ever-changing circumstances.

The peace Jesus gives is much more than a feeling; it's inseparable from His person. When Jesus promised His peace, He was responding to the disciples' concern about His leaving them and going to a place where they couldn't follow Him (13:33, 37; 14:5). That's why He told them, "Do not let your hearts be troubled and do not be afraid" (14:27). Even though they couldn't physically follow Him, He would still be with them. He promised His presence with them through the ongoing companionship of His Holy Spirit: "I will not leave you as orphans; I will come to you" (v. 18).

> **The Holy Spirit makes Jesus's peace accessible because the Spirit makes it possible for us to be *with* Jesus.**

The Holy Spirit makes Jesus's peace accessible because the Spirit makes it possible for us to be *with* Jesus in the moment and to grow in love and serenity with Him. Phillips Brooks, the author of the classic Christmas hymn "O Little Town of Bethlehem," described this increasing awareness of Jesus's presence in a letter to a friend. Brooks was enduring a challenging season when a young pastor wrote him and asked about the secret of his peace, regardless of his difficulties. Brooks responded,

> These last years have had a peace and fulness which there did not used to be. I say it in deep reverence and humility. I do not think it

> is the mere quietness of advancing age. I am sure it is not indifference to anything which I used to care for. I am sure it is a deeper knowledge and truer love of Christ. . . .
>
> I cannot tell you how personal this grows to me. He is here. He knows me and I know Him. It is no figure of speech. It is the reallest thing in the world. And every day makes it realler. And one wonders with delight what it will grow to as the years go on.³

Jesus's peace actively leads us into a relationship with Him that is marked by tenderness and even anticipation. Something good is coming, and yet somehow it's already here, breaking in like the first rays of dawn. You and I are called to live into this new reality. Jesus offers us a peace that meets us wherever we are; it's a gift we learn to unwrap as we live with Him.

More and More Grace and Peace

Peter opened his second letter with this prayer of blessing: "May God give you more and more grace and peace as you grow in your knowledge of God and Jesus our Lord" (2 Peter 1:2 NLT). Growth in Jesus's peace is to be anticipated as we live with Him. Jesus is the "good shepherd" (John 10:11) who has compassion for us when we're "harassed and helpless" (Matthew 9:36). He leads us "beside quiet waters" and offers us the rest we desperately need that "refreshes" our souls (Psalm 23:2–3). His presence with us means security and love.

Still, as we reach for the peace He offers us, we soon discover the difference between living in His peace and asking

Him to bless our already busy lives. Choices must be made. When Jesus was visiting in their home and teaching, Martha wanted Jesus to tell her sister, Mary, to help her with everything she had to do to take care of their guests. But when Mary chose to simply be near Jesus, listening at His feet, He said that she chose "what is better" (Luke 10:40–42). It wasn't that Jesus didn't care about Martha or that the things she was doing didn't matter; Jesus's time was very much in demand and He knew what it was like to have a grueling day of work in front of Him (see Mark 6:30–31). Even though Martha was doing a good thing in actively serving her guests, Jesus was pointing her to something that mattered even more. Something that would actually empower Martha in her serving others, and transform her attitude along the way.

The Bible calls Jesus the "Prince of Peace" (Isaiah 9:6). He is sovereign over it; because peace is His to give, we can't take it from Him and go our own way. Trying to grasp Jesus's peace and make it our own is a little like trying to catch a butterfly with your bare hands. Take a swipe at it and you'll miss it entirely, but be still for a moment and it will come to you. We have to learn how to place our hearts in a position of receptivity to know Jesus's peace as we go through the day.

Peace through Prayer

Throughout His Word God makes clear that peace comes increasingly as our hearts are opened to Him. Isaiah prayed,

> You will keep in perfect peace
>   all who trust in you,
>   all whose thoughts are fixed on you!
>   (26:3 NLT)

The apostle Paul explains this further: "For to set the mind on the flesh is death, but to set the mind on the Spirit is life and peace" (Romans 8:6 ESV). Paul also describes what we can do practically to live in Jesus's peace: "Do not be anxious about anything, but in every situation, by prayer and petition, with thanksgiving, present your requests to God. And the peace of God, which transcends all understanding, will guard your hearts and your minds in Christ Jesus" (Philippians 4:6–7). That word *guard* (or *garrison* is another meaning of the word in the original biblical language) describes a peace that surrounds us and keeps our hearts and minds. It is alive within us, a continual source of hope that cannot be snuffed out.

You and I are meant to discover more and more of Jesus's peace through prayer. Seven words are used to describe prayer in the New Testament, and four of them are contained in Philippians 4:6. Together they point to a way of life where prayer is a habit—not just one more thing to make us busy or something to check off our lists but a natural expression of hearts that reflect the new reality of living "in Christ Jesus" (v. 7). This has little to do with how "talkative" we are with God. We can be easily discouraged by comparing ourselves with others who "sound good" when they pray and come to the conclusion that "prayer just isn't my spiritual gift." But of all the gifts of the Spirit recorded in the New Testament (the two main lists are in Romans 12:6–8 and 1 Corinthians 12:7–11), *prayer isn't anywhere to be found.* There's a reason for this. God longs for all His children to communicate with Him from the heart.

As we do, we'll discover more of His peace.

Prayer from the Heart

In an essay entitled *The Path of Peace*, Henri Nouwen shares his experience living with and serving the severely mentally disabled at a L'Arche community. His relationships with others there helped him grasp how our hearts shape our lives in ways so basic and fundamental that we're often unaware of it happening. Writing about "the primacy of the heart," Nouwen discerned that our hearts even more than our minds help us to function in our relationships with others. This led him to conclude that our hearts (although darkened by our fallen sinfulness) best reflect our being made in the image of God, because the heart is the place within us where love dwells. Nouwen explains:

> Let me say that by the heart I do not mean the seat of human emotions in contrast to the mind as the seat of human thought. No, by heart I mean the center of our being where God has hidden the divine gifts of trust, hope and love. The mind tries to understand, grasp problems, discern different aspects of reality, and probe the mysteries of life. The heart allows us to enter into relationships and become sons and daughters of God and brothers and sisters of each other. Long before our mind is able to exercise its power, our heart is able to develop a trusting human relationship. I am convinced that this trusting human relationship even precedes the moment of our birth. Here we are touching the origin of the spiritual life.[4]

Scripture shows us continually that the condition of our hearts is what matters most to God. God reminded Samuel when he was choosing a king for Israel, "People look at the outward appearance, but the LORD looks at the heart" (1 Samuel 16:7). Jesus went there as well when he quoted Isaiah's word from God about those who "honor me with their lips, but their hearts are far from me" (Isaiah 29:13; Matthew 15:8). When we think of prayer as something that takes place only in our minds, we can easily become preoccupied with the words or particular methods we use for approaching God. But focusing on methods or words alone is like watching your feet when you're dancing; you're not really dancing until you take your eyes off yourself and turn to the one who's holding you.

Seeing prayer only as a matter of requests and answers can also get in the way of a deeper understanding of God's love for us. When answers to our prayers don't seem to come, we may mistakenly reason that God is keeping His distance from us or even that He isn't there at all. But prayer that brings peace is more than a simple transaction or linear process where input A yields output B. Prayer that brings peace is relational, a meeting of heart to heart.

> **Of all the ways we are to love God, *heart comes first*.**

When Jesus was asked which commandment was the greatest, he responded with Deuteronomy 6:5: "Love the Lord your God with all your heart and with all your soul and with all your mind" (Matthew 22:37). Of all the ways we are to love God, *heart comes first*. The Old Testament concept of "heart" that Jesus is talking about depicts the very center of human life—whatever occupies our thoughts and wills more than anything else, that which motivates us and comprises our reason for living. That's what expresses our hearts. Thus God beckons His wayward people through the prophet Jeremiah, "You will seek me and find me when you seek me with all your heart" (29:13).

Wherever you see someone walking especially close with God in Scripture, their communication with Him is straightforward and unforced. Think of Jesus using the tender Aramaic word *Abba* to speak to the Father (Mark 14:36). Or look at Abraham being candid with God that he still remained childless even though God had promised him children (Genesis 13:16; 15:3). Think about Moses begging God to see the promised land after the Lord had already told him he couldn't go in (Deuteronomy 3:23–27). All of them talked to God freely but reverently, as someone speaks with a close friend (Exodus 33:11; James 2:23). Whenever they did, they were praying from the heart.

Heartfelt prayer is grounded in the assurance that we can come to God understanding that we are fully known—faults and all—and are still deeply loved. (More on that in the next chapter.) God told His people through the prophet Joel,

> "Rend your hearts and not your
> garments."
> Return to the LORD your God,
>   for he is gracious and merciful,
>   slow to anger, and abounding in steadfast
>   love. (2:13 ESV)

God desires an inward and personal response, not something merely religious or occasional. It's the "deep calls to deep" communication that the sons of Korah wrote about in Psalm 42:7, where we come to God just as we are and pour out everything that's in us. Even more so through Jesus, God welcomes us near to His heart. In the same passage where Jesus says, "Come to me, all you who are weary and burdened, and I will give you rest," He also describes His heart: "Take my yoke upon you and learn from me, *for I am gentle and humble in heart*" (Matthew 11:28–29, emphasis added). Jesus wants us to know His heart so that we'll open our own to Him freely and unreservedly.

Being with Jesus

When an older pastor I'd known for many years was "promoted to glory," his granddaughter was one of many to celebrate his life and faith at his funeral. She reminisced about how when he would take her to the beach as a little girl, she began to notice a habit he had. He'd take off his watch and tuck it away somewhere and not look at it for the rest of the afternoon. "Why do you do that?" she asked him one day. "Because," he responded with a gentle smile, "I want you to know how important my moments with you are to me. When I'm with you, I want to just be with *you* and let time go by."

When we pray, Jesus invites us to just *be* with Him in unforced ways. Andrew Bonar observed, "We don't need to retire to the desert to meet with God. It is God who meets with us, and He can come to us at our ordinary duties."[5] We were made for this. Go back to the garden of Eden, where God is walking "in the cool of the day" and Adam and Eve hide themselves after tasting the forbidden fruit (Genesis 3:8–9). God calls to Adam, asking, "Where are you?" That question carried with it an implicit understanding that God had walked with them in the garden before, keeping company with them. If He hadn't, He wouldn't have missed their presence.

Mark also tells us that when Jesus chose the disciples, one of the main reasons he did so was "that they might *be* with him" (3:14, emphasis added). Being with Jesus changes everything. It's in being with Him—knowing that He's with us and that we're living each day in His presence—that we're able to find the peace and comfort only He can give and the strength to accomplish what we never could if left to ourselves. After Jesus rose from the dead and ascended to heaven, the religious authorities in Jerusalem saw Peter's and John's courage and "took note" that they "had been with Jesus" (Acts 4:13). Living with Him, our lives take on new purpose and power.

> **Perhaps the simplest, most practical definition of *prayer* is *being* with Jesus and living in a relationship with Him.**

A Simple Definition of Prayer

Perhaps the simplest, most practical definition of *prayer* is *being* with Jesus and living in a relationship with Him. It may involve words, but it doesn't have to. Think of an older couple who have been married for decades. There's a familiarity with each other and a gentle understanding where communication happens without saying a thing. That doesn't mean they don't interact with each other; it means there's a level of awareness where words aren't always necessary.

But this is also where the challenge lies. Jesus has promised to be "with [us] always" (Matthew 28:20), yet we need to ask ourselves, Am I *with Him*? Am I keeping company with Jesus as I go through the day? I'm grateful that His faithfulness and presence with me aren't dependent on my attentiveness (or lack thereof)—He keeps His promises even when I'm distracted. But I miss out on the peace and strength He gives if I make life all about me when larger life is right there, available and waiting. "I am the vine; you are the branches," He told His disciples. "If you do not remain in me, you are like a branch that is thrown away and withers" (John 15:5–6). Jesus holds us up and sustains us, and when we sincerely choose to try to live with Him in the moment, we discover that He "rewards those who earnestly seek him" (Hebrews 11:6).

C. S. Lewis describes what this looks like practically each day:

> It comes the very moment you wake up each morning. All your wishes and hopes for the day rush at you like wild animals. And the first job each morning consists simply in shoving them all back; in listening to that other voice, taking the other point of view, letting that other larger, stronger, quieter life come flowing in. And so on, all day. Standing back from all your natural fussings and frettings; coming in out of the wind.[6]

The "larger, stronger, quieter life" isn't something we make happen. It flows in as we open our hearts increasingly to God. When we think of being with Jesus, we may feel at a loss because we can't see or touch Him in the same way His followers did when He lived on earth physically. But according to Jesus it's a good thing that He went away because now we can know Him even more intimately.

Instead of being beside us for just three years during His earthly ministry, He can now be *within* us through the person of the Holy Spirit, living with us in a closer way than ever before. "Nevertheless, I tell you the truth: it is to your advantage that I go away, for if I do not go away, the Helper will not come to you. But if I go, I will send him to you" (John 16:7 ESV).

Now you and I can live with Jesus twenty-four hours a day. We don't tend to think of ourselves having an advantage over the disciples in this, but we do according to Jesus. And He underscored the promise of the Spirit by saying, "I have told you all this so that you may have peace in me" (v. 33 NLT). When we consider the difference the Spirit's presence makes with regard to prayer in our lives and the peace that can come from it, it's breathtaking.

Welcomed into Love

When we are "born again" (John 3:3, 7) through "the washing of rebirth and renewal by the Holy Spirit" (Titus 3:5), God not only restores a relationship with Him that was lost in Eden; He welcomes us as daughters and sons. That's why Paul wrote that "the Spirit you received does not make you slaves, so that you live in fear again; rather, the Spirit you received brought about your adoption" (Romans 8:15). God isn't holding us at arm's length, waiting to see if we're good enough to receive what He's done for us. He's beckoning us to draw near.

It follows from this that prayer was never meant to be an exercise of drudgery or discipline, if by discipline we mean something that almost seems like a punishment because we'd rather be doing something else. If I were to tell my wife, Cari, "I'm going to discipline myself to spend some time with you," she probably wouldn't take it as a compliment. How can it be a "discipline" to spend time with someone whom we love and who loves us in return? Or how can I say I love someone and have a relationship with them if I only contact them when I want something? We have to capture a fresh perspective of what it means to pray by understanding the Father's heart for us. Paul, like Jesus, points to the tenderness of this relationship at the end of the verse above when he writes, "Now we call him, 'Abba, Father'" (v. 15 NLT). The word *Abba* indicates someone to be cherished, someone we live near to and love dearly.

God welcoming us as His children isn't some dusty theological concept; it's alive with promise and intensely personal. Our Savior's kindness to us permeates our past, present, and future so completely that nothing "will be able to separate us from the love of God that is in Christ Jesus our Lord" (v. 39). Throughout God's Word, He shows us how much He deeply desires for us to be with Him. Our Father misses us when we stay away. That's the astoundingly open and generous nature of His heart for us. Through Jesus, God has run to us with open arms, and through His Spirit, He welcomes us into a relationship that's intended to keep getting better as we grow closer to Him. Even now, every longing of our hearts for Him is received with perfect love. Even here, our hearts are meant to be more and more at home with Him, living increasingly in His presence and peace.

Heaven opens here, and a growing peace beckons. Not through greater effort on our part but through letting go of ourselves a little and leaning into love.

Peace through Prayer

PURSUING PEACE

- Read Jesus's promise of peace in John 14:27 a few times, until you can say it aloud without reading it. Imagine that He is saying it to you personally. Then tell Him, "I receive your peace."
- Set aside your mobile phone and "press pause" on any distractions that you can, then take a moment to quietly be in God's presence, resting in His love for you.
- Reread C. S. Lewis's quote about letting God's "larger, stronger, quieter life" flow in. Where do you need Jesus's peace most of all? Ask Him to help you in that area of your life.

"Peace I leave with you; my peace I give you. I do not give to you as the world gives. Do not let your hearts be troubled and do not be afraid."

CHAPTER TWO

Peace with Our Past

Changed by Love

I am sure, my dear fellow servant, that life will break you unless you learn the habit of leaning on Jesus. Do not be afraid to lean too much.

Charles Haddon Spurgeon

His face was a portrait of pain. Every line on his contorted brow showed his anguish; every scar on his weathered face betrayed the loathing within. He loathed himself, and the demons inside him hated him more. They tormented him incessantly, so he cut himself and tore at his clothing and lived alone. Others lived in fear of him and tried to bind him with chains, and he despised them all the more for it. Day after day he watched the shadows lengthen around him. Night after night he thought about hurling himself over a nearby cliff into the sea. Or did that thought come from the voices inside? His struggle was so intense, the lines of his identity so blurred, that he didn't know anymore. He just knew that he wanted it all to go away.

Then the morning came. There was a boat down by the shore. A man stepped out of it and began to walk straight toward him. "When he saw Jesus, he cried out and fell at his feet, screaming at the top of his voice, 'What do you want with me, Jesus, Son of the Most High God? I beg you, don't torture me!'" (Luke 8:28). Within moments, the legion of demons that had tormented him was gone. They entered a herd of pigs nearby and drove them to their deaths into the sea.

The man once so tormented was now at peace. A serenity unlike any he had ever known filled him. He sat near Jesus; his mind was clear. He was content. In Jesus's presence, he felt something he hadn't experienced in years. There was acceptance and compassion, even love. He didn't want to be anywhere else.

Then the people came. The ones from his past. And as usual, they were filled with fear. But the loathing he once felt for them was gone. Even though they asked Jesus to leave. That doesn't matter, the man thought, I'll just go with Him.

As Jesus was stepping back into the boat, the man pleaded to go along. Jesus turned to him with a knowing but gentle look. "Go home to your own people," He said softly, "and tell them how much the Lord has done for you, and how he has had mercy on you" (Mark 5:19).

So he went. And while we don't see him again in the pages of Scripture, like ripples on a pond, the results of the impact Jesus made in his life are visible just a little later. Mark tells us that "the man went away and began to tell in the Decapolis [or Ten Cities] how much Jesus had done for him. And all the people were amazed" (v. 20). So amazed, apparently, that the next time Jesus visited that area, instead of pleading with Him to leave, a "large crowd gathered"—"about four thousand were present" (8:1, 9). And Jesus miraculously fed them all.

We don't even know his name. But could it be that this formerly broken soul that biblical scholars remember as "the Gerasene demoniac" was also one of the first missionaries? Was that the reason Jesus didn't let him go with Him in the boat, because He had a purpose for him that no one would've imagined? Could it be that the very ones who thought the man was too far gone to save were themselves brought to Jesus because of him?

Though there's much we don't know, this much we can be assured of: encountering Jesus and His love changes us, despite whatever mess we found ourselves in before. Where chaos once reigned, new hope begins to rise within us, like the sun coming up, dispelling our darkness. Because *He* cares for us, we discover that we are worth loving, despite what we may have been or done or what others may have done to us. His love goes deep, deeper even than the habits and hurts from the past that once held us captive. It overcomes old thoughts and attitudes, welcoming us into "the freedom of the glory of the children of God" (Romans 8:21 ESV). There's something about being with Jesus that gives us a peace we've never had before.

And that brings us back to prayer, and to the apostle John.

A Lavish Love

When John began to follow Jesus, he was a hotheaded fisherman. One day a Samaritan village didn't welcome

Jesus or His ministry, so John and his brother James turned to Jesus and asked Him, "Do you want us to call fire down from heaven to destroy them?" (Luke 9:54). You have to wonder where they got an idea like that—they had never heard Jesus pray like that or even insinuate it. So understandably, "Jesus turned and rebuked them" (v. 55). Perhaps that incident prompted Jesus to give them the playful nickname "Boanerges, which means 'sons of thunder'" (Mark 3:17).

But John wouldn't stay that way. Somewhere over time, the thunder softened in John's heart. You see it in the phrase he uses to describe himself five times throughout his gospel: the disciple "whom Jesus loved" (see John 13:23; 19:26; 20:2; 21:7, 20). Being with Jesus day by day so changed John that toward the end of his life he referred to what God did for us through Christ as the ultimate definition of what it means to be truly, deeply loved. "This is real love—not that we loved God, but that he loved us and sent his Son as a sacrifice to take away our sins" (1 John 4:10 NLT). John used to be a "son of thunder"; now he was a child of God.

John stood near Jesus as He gave His life for our sins on the cross (John 19:26). John also recalled Jesus's words spoken the night before in the upper room: "Greater love has no one than this: to lay down one's life for one's friends" (15:13). John understood that the best thing that ever happened to him was Jesus meeting him in his sinfulness and loving him into eternal life. Grasping the truth that God knows us completely and loves us so deeply that He willingly died a painful death so that we might be with Him forever removes any worry of His pushing us away. So John concludes with words that leap ebulliently from his transformed heart onto the page, "See what great love the Father has lavished on us, that we should be called children of God! And that is what we are!" (1 John 3:1).

It's important to remember that John wrote those words late in his life. We may think it was easier for John to communicate with Jesus because he walked and talked with Him in physical reality, but that was only for three years of Jesus's ministry. The bulk of John's life with Him was actually after Jesus ascended, through spending time with Him in prayer. Jesus established this priority during their time on earth together. Of the four gospel writers (Matthew, Mark, Luke, and John), it was John whom Jesus took with Him to pray along with Peter and James in the garden of Gethsemane. John was a witness to what Jesus prayed there, and he recorded the longest prayer that we have from Him (John 17:1–26). Read John's Revelation, and you'll also notice that he captures prayer after prayer from the worshipers in heaven. John's softened heart made him sensitive and open to being with Jesus in prayer.

> **To know God and to know we've received His forgiveness for our past wrongs is to know peace.**

God's Longing for Us

God's heart is to restore us to a relationship with Himself that's filled with peace. To know God and to know we've received His forgiveness for our past wrongs is to know peace. The Spirit poetically expressed this heartfelt desire of God for His people through the prophet Isaiah when he wrote,

> Oh, that you had listened to my
> commands!
> Then you would have had peace flowing
> like a gentle river
> and righteousness rolling over you like
> waves in the sea. (48:18 NLT)

We see this again when Jesus appeared to the disciples after the resurrection. When Jesus was arrested in the garden of Gethsemane, "everyone deserted him and fled" (Mark 14:50). We can only imagine how the disciples (who were hiding behind locked doors out of fear for their lives) must've felt when they first saw Jesus after His torturous death on the cross. They were probably wondering, What will He say to us? Will He reject us and send us away because we turned our backs on Him?

Jesus's first words must've come as a welcome relief to them: "Peace be with you!" (John 20:19). Then, as they're face-to-face with the fact that He has conquered death and it all begins to sink in, Jesus repeats Himself: "Peace be with you!" (v. 21). At this point it's more than just the usual first-century Jewish greeting. It's an assurance of all that He is and that He still loves them regardless of what happened in the past.

Getting closer to the peace Jesus wants to give us is life-altering. As we saw in the first chapter, God desires our prayers to be about so much more than just requests or answers. Prayer at its best is relational. The Creator of the universe, who spoke the stars into existence, longs deeply for us. He sought us out, even though He didn't have to. He's entirely self-sufficient and needs nothing, but He pursues us out of His absolute goodness and through no merit of our own: "While we were still sinners, Christ died for us" (Romans 5:8). Even though He could have trillions of reasons for turning us away, God chose to lavishly love us. He went to the lengths of the incarnation, the cross, and the empty tomb so we can be with Him beyond time in an eternity that opens before us here and now.

This can be hard for us to comprehend, especially when we see our faults and the sins we struggle with then and now and wonder how someone as flawless as God could want anything to do with us. John Newton, the former slaver whom God transformed to become a pastor and hymn writer, offered this solid encouragement to a young woman who was discouraged by her ongoing struggle with sin:

> [God] sees us from first to last. A thousand evils arise in our hearts, a thousand wrongnesses in our conduct, which, as they do arise, are new to ourselves, and perhaps at some times we were ready to think we were incapable of such things; but none of them are new to Him to whom past, present, and future are the same. The foresight of them did not prevent His calling us by His grace. Though He knew we were vile, and should prove ungrateful and unfaithful, yet He would be found of us; He would knock at the door of our hearts, and gain Himself an entrance.[1]

"Yet He would be found of us." God, who exists outside of time, knows the sins we'll commit even after we decide to follow Him. But that didn't stop Him from loving us. The reference Newton makes here is to the third chapter of Revelation, where Jesus tells those in the church at Laodicea, "Look! I stand at the door and knock" (v. 20 NLT). The invitation comes with a tender promise: "If you hear my voice and open the door, I will come in, and we will share a meal together as friends." The early readers of Revelation understood from their culture that the point of sharing a meal is friendship and enjoying each other's company. The "meal" Jesus refers to here is the pleasure of just being with Him. This same thought is reflected in Jesus's comment to His disciples in John 4:34 when they were urging Him to eat: "My food . . . is to do the will of him who sent me and to finish his work."

God has sought us out because He longs for us in an even more profound way than a loving parent longs for a child after a long absence. Our adversary the devil wants to rob us of the peace and joy that being with God offers us, so he strategizes against it at every level, especially pushing back against prayer. But God deeply desires to show us His goodness and draw us closer still.

This longing is something God expresses actively and repeatedly throughout His Word. When His people wandered from Him, He entreated them through the prophet Isaiah, "Yet the LORD *longs* to be gracious to you; therefore he will rise up to show you compassion" (30:18, emphasis added). This is the same longing of heart that Jesus points to when He describes the father in His parable of the prodigal son as "filled with compassion" (Luke 15:20). This phrase in the original language describes deep, internal feeling. Because of that compassion, when the father saw his son "still a long way off," he "ran to" him and "threw his arms around him and kissed him." This longing heart of the Father is for all prodigals, including those who are "a long way off" and those who (like the older brother) are trusting in their own efforts to save themselves. Jesus Himself is the personification of the running father in the parable, welcoming us to God's warm and forgiving embrace when we turn away from actively pursuing sin and come home to Him.

Scripture also shows us God's longing for us in the next to last chapter of Revelation, where we see His intentions ultimately fulfilled: "And I heard a loud voice from the throne saying, 'Look! God's dwelling place is now among the people, and he will dwell with them. They will be his people, and God himself will be with them and be their God'" (21:3). The voice coming from "the throne" indicates God speaking, looking forward to being close to those He loves, when they will be forever His and He will be theirs. And just a little earlier John shows us that our communication with God is so precious to our heavenly Father that He keeps it before Him always. The heavenly beings surrounding God's throne hold "golden bowls full of incense, which are the prayers of God's people" (5:8). Our prayers matter to God because *we* matter. Like a parent with pictures of beloved children placed prominently throughout a home, God keeps our prayers near Him because they are the expressions of hearts He longs to have close.

Leaning Prayer: Praying with John

Putting together these two thoughts of God's knowing us entirely and yet longing for us can be a great help when we pray. We can be completely open about our mess—the sins we're wrestling with, our need to love Him more, our struggles when it comes to praying—and know that we are heard with love. John assures us, "If we confess our sins, he is faithful and just and will forgive us our sins and purify us from all unrighteousness" (1 John 1:9).

John knew what he was talking about. As a "son of thunder," he no doubt had plenty of sins to confess, not only from before his life with Jesus but afterward as well (as the fire from heaven incident illustrates). But now, as the disciple "whom Jesus loved," notice how close John is to Jesus in His last days on earth. At the Last Supper, on the evening before the crucifixion, "lying back on Jesus' chest was one of His disciples, whom Jesus loved" (John 13:23 NASB). Then later at the cross, when many of the other disciples had fled and were keeping their distance, "Jesus saw his mother there, and the disciple whom he loved standing nearby" (19:26).

John longed to be close to Jesus because he understood that Jesus loved him unconditionally. John's leaning on Jesus at the Last Supper also suggests a wonderful posture of the heart when we pray. We can "lean into" Jesus because He is always near us, just as He promised, and we can receive the rest and peace He so generously offers us. This is more than just visualizing ourselves leaning on Jesus; it's an approach rooted in God's Word, which speaks of inclining our hearts toward God (Joshua 24:23; Proverbs 2:2 NASB). We lean with our hearts.

Praying like this doesn't require words as much as a simple expression of love from our hearts and the desire to be close to Him, drawing our every strength from Him. When we lean, we're trusting Him to save us and affirming that we love Him and need Him for everything. Learning to lean is immensely practical, because it helps keep us close to God throughout the day. Thus David wrote, "My soul clings to you; your right hand upholds me" (Psalm 63:8 ESV).

The language may sound sentimental, but only because it includes all that we are and doesn't rule out emotion. We can't lean, we can't "love the Lord [our] God with all [our] heart and with all [our] soul and with all [our] mind" (Matthew 22:37), without yielding everything that is in us.

We can lean into our Savior in prayer anytime, anywhere, when going about our work or sitting in a waiting room or resting our head on our pillow at night. Leaning is turning to His strength, because "he himself is our peace" (Ephesians 2:14). We receive His peace as we draw near in our hearts, confessing any sin and realizing our deep need for His saving love. "Leaning prayer" is a tenderhearted acknowledging of God's unconditional love for us. Think of a child held in a loving mother's or father's arms, rested and strengthened by the moments there. We can pray like this because we, like John, are deeply loved. We're not only fully known and accepted; we're welcomed to draw near to a love that longs to do us good for all eternity. Jesus didn't mind when John leaned. And just as Jesus longed for His friends to be with Him as He prayed in the garden of Gethsemane the night before He went to the cross, He wants to keep us close—very close—through prayer.

> **"Leaning prayer" is a tenderhearted acknowledging of God's unconditional love for us.**

Peace with Our Past

Jesus is our peace, always. We can fully entrust our past to Him and rest in the incomprehensible truth that no matter how twisted or willful our choices have been, God, with a determined and costly love, "has rescued us from the dominion of darkness and brought us into the kingdom of the Son he loves" (Colossians 1:13). Our sin once separated us from a holy and perfect God, but Paul writes about Jesus that "God was pleased to have all his fullness dwell in him, and through him to reconcile to himself all things . . . by making peace through his blood, shed on the cross" (vv. 19–20).

What He has done is *so* good that it can be hard for us to accept He would go to such lengths for us. But while we sometimes catch a glimpse of the evil we're capable of and it makes us shrink back in fear and self-loathing, God draws near to us through Jesus and wants a relationship with us. When we confess our sinfulness and receive Jesus's forgiveness offered to us at the cross, God brings peace by overcoming our past with love, giving us a new beginning and a new identity. Our past no longer defines us, even when we struggle to overcome the same sins over and over again. He never gives up on us but instead helps us live into the liberating truth that He has completely and entirely forgiven us. "If anyone is in Christ, he is a new creation. The old has passed away; . . . the new has come" (2 Corinthians 5:17 ESV). He completely "understands our weaknesses" (Hebrews 4:15 NLT) and is able to bring us through them.

When God set my son free from heroin addiction, he was surrounded by a group of believing friends who were both former addicts and shared his love of surfing. As Geoff struggled with some of the painful things that resulted from his previous choices and wondered how to go forward with his life, his friends' frequent response was, "Just come to Jesus. We'll figure the rest out later."

It took time for Geoff to take their advice to heart, but

as he did, he discovered that Jesus was faithful to lead him out of his troubled past into a future filled with hope. One of the things that frequently discouraged him was the perspective that "You're just an addict; that's all you'll ever be." Our adversary the devil used that thought to persuade him that he'd never be free from his addiction or his past failures and mistakes. But as soon as Geoff began to grasp the reality of God's love and what Jesus accomplished for him at the cross, he was won over by the soul-saving truth that "if the Son sets you free, you will be free indeed" (John 8:36 ESV). That was well over a decade ago. Today Geoff serves God as a pastor, with the intent of helping students avoid the choices he made and helping them turn to God.

Our adversary would have us stay hopelessly mired in our past and the sins we were saved from, continually living with discouragement and regret. He'd rather have us stay focused on ourselves and away from even the thought of praying, living out each day with a guilty conscience in the lands of "If only . . ." and "I wish I'd never . . . ," far from our joy in God. Whenever we start to go down those roads, we do well to heed the poet George Herbert's helpful words. In a poem titled "Conscience," he wrote about giving his thoughts this course correction:

> Peace prattler. . . .
> By listening to thy chatting fears,
> I have both lost mine eyes and ears.[2]

Herbert's point was that we must not lose sight of our Savior and what He has done for us; we must let our hearts turn to Him so that we may receive the peace He died to give us.

John no doubt faced the same struggle with a persecuted

conscience at times, and he marked the path to new freedom in Christ with these words: "This is how we know that we belong to the truth and how we set our hearts at rest in his presence: If our hearts condemn us, we know that God is greater than our hearts, and he knows everything" (1 John 3:19–20). Jesus doesn't condemn, because "there is no condemnation for those who belong" to Him (Romans 8:1 NLT). Think of His question to the woman caught in adultery about her accusers, after each one had walked away: "Woman, where are they? Has no one condemned you?" (John 8:10 ESV). He's standing right in front of her, but she clearly recognizes that He isn't condemning her, so she tells Him that all have left. His response underscores the obvious truth: "Neither do I condemn you; go, and from now on sin no more" (v. 11 ESV).

Our Savior is so much greater than our sins. He is able to take the broken shards of our past and make them a window for His light to shine through. As He puts us back together, we become stronger in the broken places, able to learn from our mistakes and point those who are struggling with the same sins to the encouragement we've found. The things we've done that we so deeply regret become reasons to love Him more, because they are forgiven. He didn't have to, but He chose to. Not because we deserve it, but because He is *that good*. We aren't who we once were—"He has removed our sins as far from us as the east is from the west" (Psalm 103:12 NLT)—and this kind of love evokes love. Remember Jesus's words about the sinful woman who wiped His feet with her hair? "Her sins—and they are many—have been forgiven, so she has shown me much love" (Luke 7:47 NLT). Those who are forgiven much love much.

Jesus longs for us with an unrelenting love, fiercely willing to face every kind of evil in order to set us free. Go back again with Him for just a moment on His journey to the Gerasenes to heal the man possessed by a legion of demons. He traveled all night to get there, staring down a storm and commanding it with a few words: "Quiet! Be still!" (Mark 4:39). As soon as He arrives, He does one thing and turns around and leaves. Jesus had to know His trip would end that way, with the locals begging Him to go. But even one shattered life was worth the effort.

Picture the man, set upon and possessed by demons, throwing himself before Jesus in agony. But there he is moments later, sitting peacefully "at Jesus' feet, fully clothed and perfectly sane" (Luke 8:35 NLT), about to be sent on a mission for God.

> **Your past isn't too much for Him.**

Your past isn't too much for Him; He will meet you with love and help you right where you are. He won't let you stay there. He has things for you to be about that you haven't discovered yet—and all of eternity to show you. He is even able to bring good that you never thought was possible from things you regret in your past, simply because He is that good.

It all starts with Him. "He is able to save to the uttermost those who draw near to God through him" (Hebrews 7:25 ESV); He is even praying for you right now. Why not lean in a little more and rest your soul in Him? He doesn't mind. He won't push you away or hold you at arm's length. He knows all about your past and loves you anyhow. Not only that, He sees who you *will be* as you stay close to Him. No matter who you once were or what you've done or what others have said about you, there's peace to be found at Jesus's feet. He longs to have you with Him, more than you could ever know.

Go ahead and lean.

PURSUING PEACE

- Read Colossians 1:13. In what ways has Jesus rescued you and changed your life? Take a little time to reflect on this and to thank Him for what He's done for you.
- Think of John leaning on Jesus. When you have the opportunity as you're sitting or lying down, imagine that you are leaning into Jesus as well. As you lean, talk to Him about anything that is on your heart.
- George Herbert's observation in his poem "Conscience" helps us take our focus off ourselves and put it on our Savior. Ask for Jesus's help to do this more.

CHAPTER THREE

Peace We Were Meant For

Running Home

*Pray so that there is a real continuity between
your prayer and your whole actual life.*

P. T. Forsyth

The moment lives in my memory in vivid color. A stunning young woman, dark from hours outdoors, sat on a rickety green playground swing set gently rocking a little boy. He was about five years old, skinny and small for his age, hair buzzed short because of the lice he once had from living on the streets. That was behind him now. Sometimes she bowed her head over him, and it looked like she was praying. As they sat there, a tear slipped from her eye and crept silently down her cheek. She wore a simple white and yellow cotton dress, and the cheerful spring sun cast a golden glow about them, as if they were caught up in a holy moment.

They were, actually. I just hadn't figured that out yet. I

stood nearby, nineteen years old and unable to look away. We had been on a college mission trip together for several days at an orphanage in Mexico. Seeing the tear, I approached them quietly and awkwardly broke the silence. "Is everything OK?" I asked. "You look, um . . . upset."

"I'm OK," she replied with a serene smile. "But my heart aches for him because tomorrow I'll go back to the States, to my family and everything I have, and he'll have to stay here. He has no family apart from this orphanage. He has nothing." She leaned forward again to give the little boy a hug, and as they rocked back and forth her words began to sink in.

I knew her well enough to know she didn't have much either, at least not in the way of material things. She and her family were refugees from an island nation with a brutal dictator who had forced her father into hard labor, which left him with a permanent disability. Once they had been wealthy and owned homes, but everything they possessed was confiscated before they left, and they came to the States with just a suitcase or two. Each member of her family had to adapt to a foreign culture, learn a new language, and start life over. And life had not been kind.

But she didn't see it that way. The way she saw it, she was deeply blessed, possessing so much that she needed to help others less fortunate than she was. Her name, Caridad (Spanish for "charity"), had been aptly chosen. Not too many years later she would become my wife. But it was in that moment at the swing set that I caught a glimpse of something within her that I couldn't forget, something that drew me in and, different as we were, somehow spoke to me of home. It took me awhile to pin it down, but once I saw it, I couldn't help loving her for it.

What I saw in her was the compassionate hospitality of Jesus.

The Hospitality of Jesus

Hospitable may not be one of the first words that comes to mind when we think of Jesus. After all, didn't He say about Himself, "Foxes have dens and birds have nests, but the Son of Man has no place to lay his head" (Matthew 8:20)? Jesus didn't have a home to call his own, so how could he possibly be hospitable?

Yet so much about Jesus speaks of home. Listen again to His words, "Come to me, all you who are weary and burdened, and I will give you rest" (11:28). He speaks with authority; there's not a doubt in His mind that He's able to do what He says. And once we begin to understand who He actually is, more comforting words were never spoken. Those words are like a signpost pointing to the One who offers "shelter and shade from the heat of the day, and a refuge and hiding place from the storm and rain" (Isaiah 4:6). Or ponder Jesus's promise, "In my Father's house are many rooms. If it were not so, would I have told you that I go to prepare a place for you? And if I go and prepare a place for you, I will come again and will take you to myself, that where I am you may be also" (John 14:2–3 ESV). What could be more welcoming than that?

This is peace that pursues us and hospitality that reaches out to pull us in. There's no one more hospitable than Jesus, because "all things were made through him" (1:3 ESV) and as a result everything in creation belongs to Him. We walk on His earth, breathe His air, and eat the food He provides. Whether we acknowledge Him or not, He generously makes everything necessary for our lives and every blessing we enjoy available to us.

Jesus offers us the soul-rest we so desperately need in a broken, stressed, and angry world. "Let me teach you," He said, "because I am humble and gentle at heart, *and you will find rest for your souls*" (Matthew 11:29 NLT, emphasis added). When life frays at the edges and unravels, He gives us a permanent place to rest. He speaks into our emptiness and meets our deepest need: "Whoever comes to me will never be hungry again. Whoever believes in me will never be thirsty" (John 6:35 NLT). Jesus isn't talking about physical hunger or thirst but the eternal soul-satisfaction that an ever-changing world can never fulfill. His invitation is both sweepingly broad and intensely personal at the same time: "Let anyone who is thirsty come to me and drink" (7:37).

Jesus's hospitality, apparent again and again throughout His life, is so generous and effusive that once you recognize it, you can't unsee it. He turned water into huge quantities of exquisite wine at a wedding in Cana (John 2:1–12). He had compassion on crowds "because they were harassed and helpless, like sheep without a shepherd" (Matthew 9:36). He welcomed children (19:14) and fed thousands of people (14:21) and even touched someone with leprosy (Luke 5:13). He planned the Last Supper in advance (22:7–14). Or consider His plea in His prayer in the upper room: "Father, I want those you have given me to be with me where I am" (John 17:24). Jesus reveals again and again that He's both "the door" (10:9 ESV) to where we belong and the "light of the world"

> **Something about Jesus feels like home.**

(8:12) that beckons us home after our long and lonely journey in the dark.

Something about all of this feels familiar, like we're being welcomed to a place where we were meant to be all along. Like puzzle pieces long lost, we fit in the picture. We belong *with Him*, and the more we get to know His kindness, the closer we want to be. We were made for this, to be near Him. Just think about Peter's words when others were turning back from following Jesus. Jesus asked him if he wanted to leave too, and Peter responded, "Lord, to whom shall we go? You have the words of eternal life" (6:68). It's almost as if he's saying, "There's no place we'd rather be, because You are the place *where we live*." Something about Jesus feels like home.

Praying Home

Seeing Jesus as our home can at first seem like an overly sentimental metaphor, but God's Word makes clear it's anything but that. Think again of the parable of the prodigal son, where turning away from sin and back to God is all about coming home. Or consider the winsome way Peter describes what it's like to know Jesus after he's walked with Him for decades: "Though you have not seen him, you love him; and even though you do not see him now, you believe in him and are filled with an inexpressible and glorious joy, for you are receiving the end result of your faith, the salvation of your souls" (1 Peter 1:8–9). This is the result of faith in Jesus that He wants all who have received Him to enjoy. According to Peter, this is what believing in Jesus is to be like, the normative experience for those who trust Him to save them.

We may not be able to see Him with our physical eyes,

but there's something so welcoming about Him that it fills us with love and longing. Our journey home isn't over yet—"then we shall see face to face" (1 Corinthians 13:12)—but He is with us along the way, and He is *enough*. Home is that place where we can rest and be content, loving and knowing we are loved. Jesus is all that and more. We can be ourselves with Him and come home to Him from wherever we have been. Even here, even now, even though our race isn't finished.

Coming to a fresh awareness of what it means to be at home with God is also beautifully freeing for the way we pray, especially if we struggle with spending any amount of time in prayer. Rosalind Rinker observed, "Prayer is the expression of the human heart in conversation with God. The more natural the prayer, the more real He becomes. . . . Prayer is a dialogue between two persons who love each other."[1]

Imagine the conversations you can have in a home where you are truly, unconditionally loved and accepted. Contrast this with the one-off approach to prayer that can happen all too often when we're in a rush. Life can get so busy, and even moments spent with God can become something we go through without much thought or feeling, matter-of-factly checking it off our lists so we can move on to the next thing as we take on the day. When we think of prayer as something we *have* to do, we may pray at meals and now and again as situations of need arise, but we feel guilty for not praying more. Yet at the same time we know that being legalistic about the time we spend with our heavenly Father in prayer isn't the answer either.

What we're missing is an outlook that sees prayer as an opportunity that's not to be missed, something we *get* to do. When we embrace the truth that we're always meant to be at home with Jesus, our praying takes on new life and purpose. We discover new peace and a sense of anticipation about being with Him. We also make the discovery that God isn't disappointed *in* us because we don't spend more time with Him in prayer; He's disappointed *for* us because of what we're missing when we try to run our lives apart from Him. "Non-discipleship," Dallas Willard pointed out, "costs abiding peace, a life penetrated throughout by love, faith that sees everything in the light of God's overriding governance for good, hopefulness that stands firm in the most discouraging of circumstances, power to do what is right and withstand the forces of evil. In short, it costs exactly that abundance of life Jesus said he came to bring (John 10:10)."[2]

The beautiful truth is that Jesus is always waiting for us, and we can be near Him at any time regardless of our feelings at the moment, learning to rest in Him and take on the adventure of life together. Ever since God "saved us through the washing of rebirth and renewal by the Holy Spirit" (Titus 3:5) and brought us into the kingdom of His Son, He welcomes us to live into a growing awareness of that reality more and more. Paul captured this relocation of our lives when he wrote, "Since, then, you have been raised with Christ, set your hearts on things above, where Christ is, seated at the right hand of God. Set your minds on things above, not on earthly things. For you died, *and your life is now hidden with Christ in God*" (Colossians 3:1–3, emphasis added). God's Spirit works like a homing beacon within our hearts, calling us to our Creator, where we belong most of all. We are meant to be at home with Him.

Jesus gets us like no one else can. We don't have to

explain ourselves with Him. He knows it all and loves us nonetheless. He died to save us so that we might be more at home with Him than we ever imagined, setting us free from our sins and self-focus to live for something more.

Jesus also modeled this "homing" behavior with the Father, spending time alone with Him every day (see Luke 5:16). We see Jesus praying in the moment, keeping in ongoing communication with His Father (see Mark 7:34; Luke 6:12). He's at home in the Father's presence wherever He is, and He longs to help us learn how to live there too.

> "Anyone who loves me will obey my teaching. My Father will love them, and we will come to them and make our home with them" (John 14:23).

A Heart at Home

Home is a place where we can lay our burdens down and be ourselves, not worrying what others think or if we're fully accepted. Jesus loves us so much that He wants us with Him here and now, loving Him back, staying close to Him through obedience. That is why He told us, "Anyone who loves me will obey my teaching. My Father will love them, and we will come to them and make our home with them" (John 14:23). What's fascinating about this promise is that Jesus isn't just describing some future point in time when He will call us to our ultimate home with Him in God's eternal kingdom (see Revelation 21:1–4). He's describing life with Him now, that He and the Father will make their home with us even before His kingdom comes, while we continue to live on this earth.

Augustine's familiar prayer sums it up this way: "You

have made us for yourself, and our hearts are restless until they rest in you."[3] The brokenness of our old ways chafes against the thought of obedience. We want to live for ourselves and be "free" without realizing that "freedom" from God leads to bondage away from what we long for most of all.

Let's go back to Jesus's words again: "Anyone who loves me will obey my teaching." Read over them too quickly and you might see one word more than any other: "Obey!" Harshness and legalism may come to mind, but that's not where Jesus is leading us. Jesus was never legalistic and wasn't thrilled when people were. Think about His encounter with a Pharisee who invited Him over for a meal. It's a large dinner party and everyone engages in the "proper" ceremonial washing of their hands before the meal. Jesus no doubt sees them, but He intentionally doesn't do it. And when His host calls Him on it, Jesus is direct: "Now you Pharisees cleanse the outside of the cup and of the dish, but inside you are full of greed and wickedness" (Luke 11:39 ESV). As always, Jesus is getting to the heart of things.

Jesus was never about rules for rules' sake. Instead, He made clear that doing what God wants us to do is a matter of love more than anything else. "As the Father has loved me," He told His disciples on their last night together, "so have I loved you. Now remain in my love" (John 15:9). We remain in His love by delighting in Him, and obedience follows. Obedience starts and ends with love. It's love that leads us to where we need to be, and because "God's love has been poured out into our hearts through the Holy Spirit, who has been given to us" (Romans 5:5), His Spirit will help us to even want what He wants. The will within us goes deep, but God's love and God's Spirit go deeper still. It is love expressed through obedience that helps us live increasingly at home with God. And in order for this to happen, we have to keep the lines of communication open with God and draw strength from Him—which means we have to pray.

This growing awareness of God's loving presence in our lives that comes as we try to love Him isn't something mystical or out of reach. It's immensely practical and sometimes not easy at all. Borrowing a parable from George MacDonald, C. S. Lewis describes God's work in our hearts this way:

> Imagine yourself as a living house. God comes in to rebuild that house. At first, perhaps, you can understand what He is doing. He is getting the drains right and stopping the leaks in the roof and so on: you knew that those jobs needed doing and so you are not surprised. But presently he starts knocking the house about in a way that hurts abominably and does not seem to make sense. What on earth is He up to? The explanation is that He is building quite a different house from the one you thought of—throwing out a new wing here, putting on an extra floor there, running up towers, making courtyards. You thought you were going to be made into a decent little cottage: but He is building a palace. He intends to come and live in it Himself.[4]

God wants to make Himself increasingly at home in our hearts, and as we go there with Him, welcoming Him into every aspect of our lives, He leads us to the discovery that "to set the mind on the Spirit is life and peace" (Romans 8:6

ESV). The more we rest in Him and loosen our insistent grip on having our own way, the more content we will become. Progress is often challenging and sometimes heartbreakingly slow, but it's genuinely possible because "he who began a good work" in us "will carry it on to completion" (Philippians 1:6). And because Jesus loves so resolutely, we can move forward in the confidence that He will never give up on us.

Obedience without love is like a tire without air—you won't get very far down the road on your own strength. Obey God just because you're following rules and you'll find yourself like the older brother in the parable of the prodigal son—miserable and maybe even angry at your Father when life doesn't give you what you feel you deserve ("Hey, I was doing everything that I should, and *this* is what happens?"). Or obey God because you are afraid of Him and you'll end up like the fearful servant in the parable of the talents, missing out on a joyful life filled with purpose and the beauty of a heartfelt relationship with Him (Matthew 25:14–30). But obey God and follow Jesus because you want to love Him back for the ways He has already loved you and true, joyful peace will follow. That's why Jesus wrapped up His command to remain in His love by saying, "I have told you this so that my joy may be in you and that your joy may be complete" (John 15:11). Then obedience becomes, as George MacDonald wrote, "the opener of eyes."[5]

Love calls us to obedience, which leads us to discover a depth of peace we never knew before.

Running Home to Love

When we genuinely love someone, we're not going to want to harm our relationship by doing something that would cause distance or hurt between us. The love God pours into us gives us the strength we need to walk more closely with Him. This is the tenderness of heart God is working within us—the "new heart" and "new spirit" that long to please Him instead of a heart that is set on its own way (Ezekiel 36:26).

When we have given in to sin or are facing temptation, letting God into the moment helps us align our perspective with His. David does this when he prays, "Create in me a clean heart, O God" (Psalm 51:10 ESV). Our closeness to God depends on this kind of vulnerable openness. "Draw near to God, and he will draw near to you," James reminds us (James 4:8 ESV).

Go way back to the garden of Eden in Genesis 3, and you find something absent from Adam and Eve's encounter with the devil. What would've happened if they had called on God and brought him into the conversation? What if Eve said, "Abba, could you come here please? There's a serpent over here, and it's telling me that if I eat this fruit that you warned me against, I won't die and I'll be like you. So, Abba, I'm confused because I want to eat it. What should I do?"

A few possible scenarios come to mind, but here's what I think would've happened. First, the devil would have made himself scarce as soon as he heard God's footsteps. Then Adam and Eve would've likely received a lesson on who the devil really is, a liar and thief who "comes only to steal and kill and destroy" (John 10:10). I don't think God would've responded, "Don't eat it because I told you so!" A more likely answer would be, "Don't eat it because I love you, and if you eat it there will be a distance between us that would be unthinkable, and oh, I don't want that for you, and you don't either. Because I am your source of life and everything good, and apart from me you'll die."

One of the most comforting things about Jesus is that He's never surprised or repulsed by our brokenness. It's the very reason that He came. He even quoted this Scripture about Himself: "A bruised reed he will not break, and a smoldering wick he will not snuff out" (Matthew 12:20; Isaiah 42:3). Letting Him into our struggle with sin is a step forward in openness with Him and maturity that He loves. Even when we think no one is watching, He's right there and knows every challenge we face. (Think of how a two-year-old plays hide-and-seek by covering her eyes and standing in the same place without hiding and you get a picture of what our "secret" thoughts look like to God.) But when we call on the Lord for help by bringing our temptations before Him, praying prayers like "I love you more than this, Lord," we open new doors for the love that He has "poured out into our hearts through the Holy Spirit" (Romans 5:5) to push all rivals away.

No temptation can stand before the expulsive power of the love that Jesus wants to fill our hearts and minds with, love that fills us and sustains us. Like a child running home when there's trouble, running home to God in our hearts helps us find the peace and protection we so desperately need.

Once asked how he resisted the devil, Martin Luther is said to have responded, "When he comes knocking upon the door of my heart and asks, 'Who lives here?' the dear Lord Jesus goes to the door and says, 'Martin Luther used to live here but he has moved out. Now I live here.' The Devil, seeing the nail-prints in His hands, and the pierced side, takes flight immediately."[6]

Jesus is our shelter who speaks to our storms, "Peace! Be still!" (Mark 4:39 ESV). Jesus is the One who goes to "prepare a place" for us (John 14:3), and even now our lives are hidden in Him. Jesus is the "way out" when we are tempted (1 Corinthians 10:13), and with Him true progress in leaving old sins behind us is possible, because "what he opens no one can shut" (Revelation 3:7). He is the One our souls yearn for long before we even realize it, the Prince of Peace who leads us home to His eternal kingdom.

No one welcomes us like Jesus. And where He is, there is joy.

The Party of Prayer

"Joy," G. K. Chesterton wrote, "is the gigantic secret of the Christian."[7] But sometimes it's a secret too well-kept in our lives, and God doesn't want it to be that way. In the same chapter of God's Word where we find the homecoming of the prodigal son, we find two other parables about a lost sheep and a lost coin. They all share something in common. In each one, when what was lost is restored to where it belongs, there's a party. The man who finds his sheep "joyfully puts it on his shoulders," and then he "calls his friends and neighbors together and says, 'Rejoice with me'" (Luke 15:5–6). The woman who finds the lost coin says the same thing: "Rejoice with me" (v. 9). And when the prodigal son comes home, "they began to celebrate" (v. 24). Jesus places this explanation in the father's words to the killjoy older brother: "But we *had to* celebrate and be glad, because this brother of yours was dead and is alive again; he was lost and is found" (v. 32, emphasis added).

God doesn't *have* to do anything, in the regard that no one can force Him to do their will. But here you see the father who represents God in the parable being so compelled by love that he can't do anything else. Behind all of this is a picture of a party that God longs for us to attend. He wants us to celebrate that we were once lost and now we're found, and He hopes that we'll join in the dance with Him as the One who is happy that He has found us. God's Word reminds us that, "for *the joy* that was set before him," Jesus "endured the cross, despising the shame, and is seated at the right hand of the throne of God" (Hebrews 12:2 ESV, emphasis added). Hidden behind the agony of the cross is a depth of joy that we can only begin to fathom. God has made a way for us to be at home with Him forever, and the joy is worth every cost.

> **God has made a way for us to be at home with Him forever, and the joy is worth every cost.**

There's a reason that there are more prayers of praise in the Bible than any other kind of prayer[8]—knowing God as our Father and Savior is the best thing that could ever happen to us. I don't know about you, but sometimes when I pray, I forget this and don't celebrate Him enough. It's as if God is there at the party holding out His arms to me in love, but I'm just standing there lost in self-focus, staring at my shoes. But when our lives are caught up in His love, our minds aren't as occupied by our failings and our problems. We think less about ourselves (except maybe about how blessed we are), more about the amazing God who loves us, and more about others. We're also better representatives to others of the good news that they so desperately need and that we've been called to share.

"Being at the party" means learning to let ourselves

celebrate God in simple and even childlike ways. While I was writing these words, my wife, Cari, brought me a warm slice of chocolate banana bread right out of the oven with a glass of cold milk. As she turned and closed the door, I lifted the glass with a broad smile in a toast to God. Silly? Perhaps, but is that such a bad thing? There was love expressed in that moment that was just between us, a simple way of thanking the Giver of "every good and perfect gift" (James 1:17) from the heart.

One day not long ago, Cari was dropping off some items at a thrift store when she noticed a woman walking down the sidewalk toward her. The woman was singing and stopped to look at a flower. She looked so happy, Cari couldn't help smiling. Then the woman's eyes met hers. "I can tell just from looking at you that you have a relationship with God," she said. Cari laughed and said, "Yes, I do." The woman shuffled her feet in a little dance and pointed skyward. "I'll see you up there," she responded.

Scripture assures us that God's people are meant for this kind of joy: "But for you who fear my name, the Sun of Righteousness will rise with healing in his wings. And you will go free, leaping with joy like calves let out to pasture" (Malachi 4:2 NLT). Calves set free from a stall will frolic and kick up their heels for the sheer joy of life. It doesn't hurt us to kick up our heels a little to celebrate the Savior who has set us free. Actually, it helps considerably.

Just because we've come home to the party doesn't mean that our lives will be without trouble. But when they're difficult, a heart at home in God's joy results in peace and hope for the future, because He reminds us that challenging seasons won't last forever, but His love will.

Eugene Peterson depicts this outlook on life in *The Message* version of Romans 8:15–17: "This resurrection life you received from God is not a timid, grave-tending life. It's adventurously expectant, greeting God with a childlike 'What's next, Papa?' God's Spirit touches our spirits and confirms who we really are. We know who he is, and we know who we are: Father and children. And we know we are going to get what's coming to us—an unbelievable inheritance! We go through exactly what Christ goes through. If we go through the hard times with him, then we're certainly going to go through the good times with him!"

Ask yourself, How do I celebrate the One who loves me so much that He died for me? How am I at home in His presence through prayer, just enjoying His company? Is finding joy in Him part of my life every day? We need to be intentional about this and ask for God's help to live there more and more. G. K. Chesterton quipped,

> You say grace before meals.
> All right.
> But I say grace before . . . sketching,
>   painting,
> Swimming, fencing, boxing, walking, playing, dancing;
> And grace before I dip the pen in the ink.[9]

Sometimes you may find yourself celebrating God in ways that are uniquely "you," ways that others may not understand. King David's wife Michal didn't get it when he danced before the Lord (2 Samuel 6:14–16). But what others think doesn't matter because God will understand, and even a moment spent in His joy is worth it.

PURSUING PEACE

- Read Luke 15:32, and thank God for His deep desire to have you near Him.
- Where are the places in your life you struggle most with temptation? Talk with Jesus about them, and ask Him to help you turn to Him the instant you are tempted, so that you may receive His strength and peace.
- In what simple, playful, or childlike way might you celebrate God's generous love for you today? Ask Him to help you to worship Him from the heart.

CHAPTER FOUR

Peace in Our Worries

Casting Cares

Angels can fly because they can take themselves lightly.
G. K. Chesterton

I don't float. I've tried, all my life. And my wife, who floats effortlessly, finds it both amusing and exasperating. "Just relax," she tells me. "You're too tense and you need to loosen up." I lean back in the water and relax as much as I can, trusting myself to buoyancy. Then I sink like a cinder block. All because I'm part of a subset of the population for whom floating in fresh water without holding my breath is physiologically nearly impossible.

I know. It doesn't sound right. As you read these words you may be shaking your head, thinking, No, not *impossible*—anyone can float if they just try hard enough. But please bear with me and I'll explain.

When I was a kid, floating was serious business, and I had a number of swimming instructors at the local pool who couldn't understand why I didn't float either. To a six-year-old, they made it seem like all I had to do was lie back, get loose, think happy thoughts, and I'd be as light as Peter Pan. But I kept sinking. Each of them tried in succession and failed one by one, until they were frustrated and I was seriously stressed out. But sternly yelling at a little kid and telling him to "Relax!" doesn't exactly have the desired effect.

Then it was Dad's turn. Dad kept going when the others had given up. He held his arms out to me in the shallow end of a neighbor's pool. With a little coaxing, I'd climb into his arms.

"Trust me, James. It'll be OK."

Then came those words: "We're just going to go out a little deeper."

"No, I don't want to!"

Dad knew I had to calm down to get anywhere, but he also knew I had reason to be tense. I was a skinny kid and my long, lead-pipe legs pulled me under every time. But then Dad said something my hapless instructors could never say, something that really helped: "I've got you. I won't let you go under. I love you and I'm right here. You can trust me."

I made progress with Dad. Even though I never was quite able to float, he did teach me to relax enough in the water so I could learn how to swim, and I still love to do it. But if I don't kick enough, my legs still sink like concrete.

If you're starting to suspect an analogy is coming, you'd be right. Living in Jesus's peace when we're tense and worried to begin with is a challenging thing. Sure, we wish we could float above troubling situations the way some people seem to do, but we may be put together in a way that life's circumstances weigh on us, pulling us down, and we just can't let go of them. Add to that the weight of others' worries because we love them and care about what happens to them and you have a recipe for borrowing trouble. Someone sternly telling us to "relax and pray more" doesn't help. But what *does* help is understanding that there's Someone to hold us up and get us through no matter how deep the water gets.

And no one knows more about that than Peter.

Walking Back to the Boat

You've probably heard the story before. Right after Jesus fed five thousand people, Matthew tells us that He "made the disciples" get into a boat and go on ahead of Him to their next spot across the lake. After that, He sends the crowd home and "went up on a mountainside by himself to pray" (14:22–23). Think of it as Jesus "putting the kids to bed" so He can have a moment alone to talk with the Father. Time on His own with the Father is vital to Jesus, so He carves out time in His schedule to make it a priority. After that, it's a bit of a walk across the water (nothing for Jesus) to where the disciples are in the boat. By now it's almost dawn, there's just enough light to barely see by, and the wind is whipping up the water and pushing hard against the boat as the disciples strain at the oars.

When they see Jesus (or at least His silhouette) out on the water, they're spooked. "'It's a ghost,' they said, and cried out in fear" (v. 26). To be fair, if you'd never heard of anyone walking on water before (they hadn't) and were exhausted because you'd been rowing all night, don't you think you might react the same way? Chances are it would freak out even the most experienced sailor.

Now comes the familiar part. After Jesus identifies Himself and tells the disciples not to be frightened, Peter says something surprising: "Lord, *if it's you* . . . tell me to come to you on the water" (v. 28, emphasis added). But why would he ask that? Peter clearly isn't convinced yet. He's not sure who it is, so he asks for more proof. But Jesus doesn't mind the request, and the way He answers it makes you catch your breath at the very first step. Peter does something unique in human history. No one besides Jesus has ever walked on water—no one except for Peter. So even though his request isn't exactly filled with faith, Jesus takes him up on it. Sometimes even impulsive prayers get astounding answers.

Pause just long enough to savor that moment. There's Peter, taking step after step on the water, sensing supernatural buoyancy and feeling the foam between his toes. Sure, we could sit back and criticize him for taking his eyes off Jesus, but there are eleven others in the boat who don't even take a step and are looking on in wonder right before his epic fail. Peter should at least get credit for trying. And from what Matthew tells us, he went quite a ways. Jesus is enough of a distance from the boat that the disciples have a hard time recognizing Him. But at the point that Peter takes his eyes off Jesus and cries out "Lord, save me!" as he's starting to sink, eyewitness Matthew writes that "*immediately* Jesus reached out his hand and caught

> **Just a little faith calmly and quietly placed in the person of Jesus can be used by God to accomplish things we never thought were possible.**

him" (vv. 30–31, emphasis added). Don't miss that. All Jesus had to do was reach. Peter almost made it all the way. That's awe-inspiring.

We also don't want to miss what Jesus said to Peter as soon as He pulled him up out of the water: "You of little faith, . . . why did you doubt?" (v. 31). Sure, those words are a rebuke, but there's something in them that can make a difference on those days when we're struggling with distraction and worry. Even with just a little faith, Peter walked on water. Just a little faith calmly and quietly placed in the person of Jesus can be used by God to accomplish things we never thought were possible.

There's even more encouragement between the lines. What happened after Jesus pulled Peter up? Matthew doesn't say that Peter swam the distance; he simply writes that Jesus "caught him" (v. 31). The word in the original language means to "grasp" or "take hold." So it's safe to reason that Jesus *pulled Peter back up out of the water*. And that would mean that after Peter tried and failed, he walked on water again. Maybe he held on to Jesus, but it's clear enough that he went the rest of the way. He found faith again. And this time there was no looking around. He stayed close to Jesus and made it all the way back to the boat.

Faith, Prayer, and Casting Cares

Taking these moments from Peter's life to heart can help us when we're struggling to put one foot in front of the other and walk by faith. "We have this treasure in jars of clay" (2 Corinthians 4:7), and it isn't always easy to be consistent. Sometimes we flail about and feel like we're getting nowhere. We take our eyes off Jesus, sink into our worries, and go down. A friend confided recently, "I spend time gazing at my worries but only glancing at Jesus, and it needs to be the other way around."

The good news is Jesus is closer than we think. Cry out to Him, and He will lift us up and help us get back on our feet to places of faith that just a little earlier seemed hopelessly out of reach. However great the anxiety we may be feeling, He can handle it. Even if we feel like we have just a "little faith," barely enough to get by, it is more than we realize because it's faith placed in Jesus, and He won't give up on us. Peter's own words written a few years later capture what it means to live dependently on Him in prayer: "Cast all your anxiety on him because he cares for you" (1 Peter 5:7).

> **Give Jesus everything you possibly can: all the fear, all the emotion, all the harshness of whatever you're up against. . . . It's not too heavy for Him to carry.**

Notice the progression of thought in that sentence. First, that word "cast." Peter the fisherman describes putting out a net. It's an intentional throwing, letting something go so that you no longer bear the full weight of it. Then, that phrase "all your anxiety." Not just some. Give Jesus everything you possibly can: all the fear, all the emotion, all the harshness of whatever you're up against, including the questioning if He's really there. It's not too heavy for Him to carry. He wants us to give it to Him because He cares that deeply. And in the honesty of that exchange between our heart and His, something precious is won. Our relationship with God deepens, and new trust flourishes that will help us receive His peace more easily the next time challenges come. There's a growing in the knowing that He has been faithful in the past, so we can lean back and loosen our grip, accepting that He won't let us go. He *has* us, and we have been loved and received by Him, and that's what matters most of all.

It isn't blind faith that everything will work out the way we want. It's the calm assurance of relationship that Paul described when he wrote, "I have learned the secret of being content in any and every situation, whether well fed or hungry, whether living in plenty or in want. I can do all this *through him* who gives me strength" (Philippians 4:12–13, emphasis added).

Mountain-Moving, Tree-Flying Faith

Sometimes we think of faith in all-or-nothing terms—as if we either have it or don't have it. But Scripture shows us that faith is something we are continually growing into. Think of the disciples telling Jesus, "Increase our faith!" (Luke 17:5), or the man with the demon-possessed son who pleaded with Him, "I do believe; help me overcome my unbelief!" (Mark 9:24). Each was an instance where they were saying, "We don't have enough faith!" And Jesus had an encouraging response on both occasions. For the disciples, He answered by describing faith in almost minuscule terms: "If you have faith as small as a mustard seed, you can say to this mulberry tree, 'Be uprooted and planted in the sea,' and it will obey you" (Luke 17:6). For the struggling father (who had already seen the disciples try to cast the demon out of his son and fail), Jesus responded not by criticizing him for any lack of faith on his part but instead by healing his son and setting him free (Mark 9:25–27).

Jesus's responses here show us something vital. Practical faith, like prayer, functions best in relationship. Our faith isn't ultimately about what we'd like to see happen or our ability to muster conviction, but rather it's in a *Person*. The smallest amount of faith placed in our Savior is an immensely powerful thing. As the angel Gabriel told Mary when he announced the birth of Jesus, "Nothing will be impossible with God" (Luke 1:37 ESV). But our relationship with God is key. Even when we struggle to believe, He understands our difficulties and wants to help us, because belief in Him expressing itself in love is what He desires most of all.

Grasping this can be challenging when God allows things to happen that we can't understand. When crises come and the thing we're praying *won't* happen does, or when a prayer about something we believe God also wants goes unanswered for years, we can easily wonder how a good and loving God could allow it.

I recently spoke to a group at a church, and there was a Q&A session afterward. One woman asked, "I had a friend whose husband was struggling with an illness. She believed that if she just had enough faith, her husband would be healed. And she didn't want to think about any other possibility, because she didn't want anything to detract from her faith that God would make him better. But God didn't heal him in the way that she was asking, and afterward she was so hard on herself, because she felt like if only she had had *more* faith, he would have been healed. What do you say to a person like that?"

It's an excellent question, one where the insufficiency of words becomes immediately apparent. Ours is a broken world where both miracles and tragedies occur, and God's wisdom and will are so often beyond our grasp to think through or articulate. But when Jesus "did not do many miracles" in his hometown "because of their lack of faith" (Matthew 13:58), it was disbelief *in Him* that was the main issue. "They took offense *at him*" (v. 57, emphasis added); thus it was their relationship with Him that defined their faith. This realization can be amazingly freeing for us when we're trying to find peace amid difficult circumstances. If our faith is only in outcomes—the things we want to see in answer to our prayers—and not in God Himself, we miss something of incalculable worth.

The Very Great Reward

We see this same focus on outcomes in Abraham's life. We tend to only think of Abraham as a man of exemplary faith. After all, "Abraham believed God, and it was credited to him as righteousness" (Romans 4:3); Abraham was so close to God that he was "called God's friend" (James 2:23). But what we can all too easily miss is that it took him awhile to get there, because we see his life after the fact. Abraham's relationship with God and his ability to trust Him took time.

Scripture is incredibly honest about this. When Abraham was still called Abram, God promised him so many descendants that He would make him "a great nation" and his "offspring like the dust of the earth" (Genesis 12:2; 13:16). But decades passed without children, and it weighed on Abram. We see this when God later tells him in a vision, "Do not be afraid, Abram. I am your shield, your very great reward," and Abram responds, "Sovereign Lord, what can you give me since I remain childless . . . ?" (15:1–2).

Stop right there. Do you see that? That's doubt, or at the very least disappointment wrapped in a question that seems very much like a complaint. Notice where Abram's focus is. The living God, the Creator of heaven and earth, has just told him, "I am your shield, your very great reward." But instead of falling down in loving admiration and worship, Abram asks, "What can you give me?" Not exactly his best moment. But what does God do in response? Does He rebuke Abram for his self-focus or say, "Don't you believe me, Abram? Where's your faith?" Not at all. This time, God lifts his eyes to a new place.

God takes Abram outside and says, "Look up at the sky and count the stars—if indeed you can count them. . . . So shall your offspring be" (v. 5). God shifts Abram's gaze from the dust to the stars. Maybe it's a way of pointing him to His grandeur, but whatever God's reasons may have been, Scripture tells us that "Abram believed the LORD" (v. 6).

Still, Abram is human like the rest of us and continues to struggle. When his wife, Sarai, tells him, "The LORD has kept me from having children" (16:2), they decide together to take matters into their own hands, and Sarai gives him her servant Hagar to start a family. Yet in spite of their willfulness, God doesn't give up on them. By now Abram and Sarai are old. But it's then, when it's clear that they can't fulfill God's promises on their own, that God changes Abram's name to Abraham (which means "father of many") and Sarai's name to Sarah ("princess"), and He reaffirms the promises He made. But when He does, Abraham "laughed and said to himself, 'Will a son be born to a man a hundred years old?'" (17:17). But God doubles down and insists that he and his wife will indeed have a baby. God even gives them the name, which is rich with meaning given their conversation and the long road they had been on together: Isaac means "he laughs."

What's encouraging about Abraham's story is that God

meets him even in his worries that he and Sarah will never have a child together. Scripture is clear on the fact that Abraham "believed the LORD" (15:6), even though a lot of questioning and some bad choices happened afterward. His faith grew over the years as he encountered God's faithfulness. And knowing that can help us as we learn how to pray and grow in trust with Him as well.

Between the Way Things Are and the Way They Ought to Be

The hardest part about having faith is living between the way things are and the way they ought to be. But it's in that in-between place that we meet God and discover that He was where we were meant to be all along. He came to this earth to be known by us. He longs to be our "shield" and our "very great reward," just as He was for Abraham. Our trust in Him isn't based on our circumstances. It has to go deeper, otherwise we will simply measure His goodness by the things that happen to us for good or ill: if times are good then God is good, but if times are bad we're not so sure. Above it and through it all, God deeply desires to meet us in our circumstances so He can draw us closer to Himself.

Oswald Chambers observed,

> We must pour into the bosom of God the cares which give us pain and anxiety in order that He may solve for us, and before us, the difficulties which we cannot solve. We injure our spiritual life when we dump the whole thing down before God and say—You do it. That spirit is blind to the real union with God. We must dump ourselves down in the

midst of our problems and watch God solve them for us. "But I have no faith"—bring your problems to God and stay with Him while He solves them, then God Himself and the solution of your problems will be for ever your own. If we could see the floor of God's immediate presence, we would find it strewn with the "toys" of God's children who have said—This is broken, I can't play with it any more, please give me another present. Only one in a thousand sits down in the midst of it all and says—I will watch my Father mend this.[1]

My wife and I encountered this truth when our son was at his deepest point of heroin addiction. He lived hundreds of miles away in another state, and our only connection was an occasional phone call. Like any addict, he was doing anything he could to feed the dragon within, stealing what he could to survive, betraying friendships, sharing needles. He was a skeleton of his former self; his drug habit had consumed so much of his winsome and loving personality that he was scarcely discernible from the person we once knew. Our hearts ached for him. We wanted to reach into his life and set things right, but that was beyond our grasp. He was an adult and responsible for his own choices, and he wanted to keep us at a distance. Every day we feared the worst, catching our breath when the phone rang, never knowing what kind of news would meet us.

The situation drove us to our knees again and again. But even putting it that way sounds more pious than it was. Some days our prayers felt like Gideon's response when the angel of the Lord told him, "The LORD is with you." Gideon answered, "If the LORD is with us, why has all this happened to us?" (Judges 6:12–13). A large part of our world came crashing down and we felt like failures as parents, haunted by the thought, "If only we had done something differently . . ." The parents of prodigals know this feeling all too well, even though their sons and daughters make their own choices—choices they never would've made themselves. Sometimes it's hard to see beyond those places that make our hearts hurt, especially in matters of life and death with someone we love. We need God to lift our sight above the pain.

Still, as Cari and I both kept praying day by day, we found that God met us. Some days ideas would come that helped us help our son, especially on days when we fasted together. (We would skip lunch on Thursdays and take extra time to pray for both our kids.) Other days nothing seemed to happen, as if "the skies above [were] as unyielding as bronze" (Deuteronomy 28:23 NLT). But it only *felt* that way. In reality, God was nearer than we thought, and over time we discovered the quiet truth Jesus described: "I am the good shepherd; I know my sheep and my sheep know me" (John 10:14). There in our pain and worry about our son, we were drawn to God's goodness and couldn't stay away.

Our Very Great Reward

As we continued to cast our cares on Him, Jesus comforted our frazzled hearts and gave us new strength, showing us that there was no better place for us to be than close to Him. Only there could we find the peace we needed.[2] "Jesus *has* come," one theologian who knew what it's like to suffer wrote. "He has overcome the anxiety which besets the world (John 16:33). He has ascended and he reigns. Faith overcomes the world not because faith is a stubborn posture over against the world but because it trusts him who has overcome and now is ruler of all."³ This is the remedy for giving our cares to God and not yanking them back again.

Our ultimate goal isn't to be rid of our problems, as relieving as that might seem. It is, instead, to be close to Jesus. And our problems offer us that opportunity. The more time Cari and I spent with Him because we *had* to, casting our desperate cares on Him, the more He became our "very great reward." In an unexpected spiritual jujitsu, as our pain and our worries drove us to prayer, God turned them to good by bringing us into an increasingly practical awareness that our relationship with Him was what mattered most of all. Even though we had long believed that, now we were in a place where we had to live there just to get through the day. Think of when God told Moses, "My Presence will go with you, and I will give you rest." And Moses responded, "If your Presence does not go with us, do not send us up from here" (Exodus 33:14–15). There simply was no other place to be. There was no better place, either. It's easier to live with Him than it is to live with worry.

God is infinitely able to use even heartbreaking situations to draw us closer to Him. It was when Paul was suffering in prison that he wrote, "I know *whom* I have believed"

(2 Timothy 1:12, emphasis added)—not "*what* I have believed." His hope was in God more than anything else, including any answers to prayer. But this is also a truth that's "discerned only through the Spirit" (1 Corinthians 2:14), and sometimes He uses life's unexpected turns to take us there. As the poet and believer William Cowper wrote, "God is his own interpreter, and he will make it plain."[4] Our part is to keep coming back to Him, leaning into Him with our worries, and placing ourselves before Him so that we may receive more of His peace. This is the faith that overcomes the world, the faith God longs to give us.

As the Scottish philosopher and pastor P. T. Forsyth observed,

> The reality of prayer is bound up with the reality and intimacy of life.
>
> And its great object is to get home as we are to God as He is. . . . The prayer of faith does not mean a prayer absolutely sure that it will receive what it asks. That is not faith. Faith is the attitude of soul and self to God which is the root and reservoir of prayer apart from all answer. It is what turns need into request. It is what moves your need to need God. It is what makes you sure your prayer is heard and stored, whether granted or not. "He putteth all my tears in His bottle." God has old prayers of yours long maturing by Him. What wine you will drink with Him in His kingdom! Faith is sure that God refuses with a smile; that He says No in the spirit of Yes, and He

gives or refuses always in Christ, our Great Amen. And better prayers are stirred by the presence of the Deliverer than even by the need of deliverance.[5]

God Himself is the best Answer to prayer long after answers have come, and even if they have not come at all, and at every point in between. Trust results as we cast our cares on Him, not because we always receive the answers we desire but because He gives of Himself. He always has. Receive of Him intentionally, and we will find strength to surpass every worry. "My heart trusts in Him, and I am helped," David discovered (Psalm 28:7 NASB). Bernard of Clairvaux discerned the same truth, closer still through the presence of Jesus:

> Jesus, Thou Joy of loving hearts,
> Thou Fount of life, Thou Light of men,
> From the best bliss that earth imparts,
> We turn unfilled to Thee again.[6]

In the "already but not yet" in which we live—the moments when we long to see our Savior face-to-face but through the comfort of His Spirit somehow know His presence still—Jesus is everything. He came to fill the in-between places with His love and life and so becomes our Peace in every worry. We cast our cares on Him not so that we can get on with our lives but because His love "is better than life" (Psalm 63:3). He is "the God of hope" who is able to fill us "with all joy and peace" as we "trust in him, so that [we] may overflow with hope by the power of the Holy Spirit" (Romans 15:13).

Our lives are better off in His hands than in our own.

PURSUING PEACE

- What cares do you need to cast on Jesus right now? As you pray about them, open your hands for each one, and ask Him to help you with them.
- Ask Jesus to help you trust Him daily with your cares, and thank Him that He is greater than anything you face.
- Read Philippians 4:6–7. Thank God that He is able to meet you in your worries and to replace them with His peace.

CHAPTER FIVE

Peace and Rest
Carried by God

*A calm hour with God is worth a
whole lifetime with man.*

R. Murray M'Cheyne

"I'd like to pray for you every day for the next thirty days," my new friend offered generously.

"Do I seem that stressed out to you?"

He smiled and kindly overlooked my awkward attempt at humor. "I'd also like to ask you to pray for me."

Some years back I attended a retreat with a pastor and author on prayer I admired. I was going through a challenging season and took the time away because I really *was* overwhelmed and stressed out with a frenetic schedule at work and challenges at home. The pastor and I became friends, and one day after a long conversation he suggested that we pray Ephesians 3:14–21 for each other daily for the next month.

That passage contains one of the great prayers of Scripture:

> For this reason I kneel before the Father, from whom every family in heaven and on earth derives its name. I pray that out of his glorious riches he may strengthen you with power through his Spirit in your inner being, so that Christ may dwell in your hearts through faith. And I pray that you, being rooted and established in love, may have power, together with all the Lord's holy people, to grasp how wide and long and high and deep is the love of Christ, and to know this love that surpasses knowledge—that you may be filled to the measure of all the fullness of God.
>
> Now to him who is able to do immeasurably more than all we ask or imagine, according to his power that is at work within us, to him be glory in the church and in Christ Jesus throughout all generations, for ever and ever! Amen.

I returned home and began to pray those words for my new friend. As I went over them again and again, God helped me commit them to memory and take them to heart. I found new comfort in their meaning day by day. And then something happened.

I got sick. At that same conference I had contracted a waterborne microorganism and began to lose weight rapidly. After I lost nearly forty pounds, on my doctor's advice my wife drove me to the local hospital and checked me in. When the wait seemed too long, I tried to leave, rationalizing that I wasn't that sick and had too many things to do.

But I was sicker than I was willing to admit and ended up stuck in a hospital bed for several days.

Still, I kept trying to pray that passage of Scripture. Sometimes the thought occurred to me: See where your prayers get you? But it didn't last long. As I was forced to rest and lie still, God's presence became real to me in a new and tender way. I wasn't only resting physically; God was showing me what it means to rest spiritually. There was a beauty about those moments that I never expected. I was too weak to push or plan or do anything, but it was then it became evident that God was teaching me a new way to live.

> **Resting causes us to consider who is ultimately in control of our lives.**

Choosing to Rest

We have to learn to rest in God if we are going to know His peace consistently in our lives. Resting in Him involves several ways to pray we've already considered: being mindful of Jesus moment by moment, leaning into Him for strength, running to Him when we're tempted, casting our cares on Him. But also resting causes us to consider who is ultimately in control of our lives. When we rest in God, He helps us learn to move at His wise pace instead of the frenzied tempo of the world around us. Resting is, in that sense, "leaning long term." It's prayer not as a lifeline but as a lifestyle; it's the dependence exemplified by Jesus, who never seemed to be in a hurry and "often withdrew to lonely places and prayed" (Luke 5:16).

How can rest be possible when we're already so busy? The good news is that resting isn't one more thing to add to our to-do list. Resting in God isn't just a position of the heart we turn to now and then; it's a posture that is learned over time. When we rest, our awareness of the depth of our need for God increases and we learn new habits for living. Resting isn't only about throttling back on how we schedule life, but it also causes us to ask vital questions: Why am I doing the things I'm doing? Am I doing them for me or for God? God's Word maps out this crossroads in our lives:

> Stand at the crossroads and look;
> > ask for the ancient paths,
> ask where the good way is, and walk in it,
> > and you will find rest for your souls.
> > > (Jeremiah 6:16)

Sadly, that passage doesn't end well. It concludes: "But you said, 'We will not walk in it.'" God's words through Jeremiah help us to see that He wants us to know His rest, and that finding it starts with asking Him for it and then following where He leads. But that will challenge us to make changes, to make the sometimes difficult choice of letting Him into our schedules so we can increasingly give Him all of them. The prophet Isaiah expressed a similar invitation from God:

> God has told his people,
> "Here is a place of rest;
> > let the weary rest here.
> This is a place of quiet rest."
> > (Isaiah 28:12 NLT)

Again, the verse finishes with the same outcome as before: "But they would not listen." Sometimes we move so quickly through life that we miss the peace God wants to give us.

Resting is, after all, something we choose to do. We choose to lie down, to go to bed at night, or to take a nap because we know we need to. Deciding to rest in God means choosing to move at His pace, walking through the day "in step with the Spirit" (Galatians 5:25). We might want to push back: Sure, that all sounds so good, but I have young kids at home and a job on top of that, and everyone wants a piece of me, and it's all I can do to just get to the end of the day! That's a reasonable response—one that brings us back to the peace God gives us when we pray.

Rest, Work, and Prayer

"Return to your rest, my soul, for the LORD has been good to you," wrote the author of Psalm 116 (v. 7). Why is the psalmist able to rest in God? Because God heard his prayer. "Because he bends down to listen, I will pray as long as I have breath!" (v. 2 NLT). Resting in God doesn't mean being idle or asleep in Him, like those who are inattentive to God, willfully going their own way and living for themselves (Romans 13:11–12; Revelation 3:2). When we are resting in Him in the positive ways His Word describes, we are intentionally close. To rest in God means that we're attentive to Him and His goodness so that He can restore our souls and direct our lives.

Still, even though it's found throughout Scripture, this idea of resting in God may not feel right, especially in a culture that highly values getting things done. How can we rest when there's so much to do—work for others, work for God's kingdom? Doesn't Jesus tell a parable about a "wicked, lazy servant" who doesn't do the work he should

(Matthew 25:26)? Didn't Jesus say, "We must do the works of him who sent me" (John 9:4)? Of course. But all the while Jesus demonstrated an ongoing, open communication with the Father, saying that He "can do nothing by himself" (John 5:19) and teaching His disciples to "always pray and not give up" (Luke 18:1).

If we rest in God *while* we work, it results in more spiritual productivity and less busyness as we move in His strength and not our own. To rest in Him is to dwell in Him and have access to everything good that He wants to give us. To rest is to remain in Him, to be still before Him, to abide. "If you remain in me and I in you," Jesus assures us, "you will bear much fruit; apart from me you can do nothing" (John 15:5).

> **Resting is about the posture of our hearts, not about expenditure of effort.**

Jesus wants us to rest in Him and to draw strength from Him continually. We can rest in Him anytime, anywhere. It may be as simple as praying His name, saying "Jesus" with a breath in or out as we go about the day. It may be praying "Jesus, I rest in you" wherever we are. Resting prayer also happens without words. Again, resting is about the posture of our hearts, not about expenditure of effort. It's more about being than doing, acknowledging by faith that God actually is with us and that we are with Him. It's simple affection in God's direction, where nothing matters more than being with Him.

Staying close like this—not through pushing hard to pray but through praying by letting go of our own strength to receive Christ's—is the "secret" Paul discloses when he writes about being "content whatever the circumstances" (Philippians 4:11). You may sometimes hear this referred to as "practicing the presence of God,"[1] but even the word *practice* places too much emphasis on ourselves and our effort. It's a giving up of self-emphasis so that we may receive from God more of His presence and peace. It's through His loving acceptance that we are able to "set our hearts at rest in his presence" (1 John 3:19). Resting in Him also enables us to listen to His Word and hear Him better, because we are naturally more focused and less distracted. It enables us to pray Samuel's prayer, "Speak, for your servant is listening" (1 Samuel 3:10), and wait quietly for His response.

Carried by God

This reality of God's rest for our hearts is directly related to the concept of God as our refuge, something we see again and again throughout Scripture. Think of the words of Psalm 46:1–2:

> God is our refuge and strength,
>   an ever-present help in trouble.
> Therefore we will not fear, though the
>   earth give way.

The authors of that psalm were the sons of Korah, descendants of a man who had led a rebellion against God and Moses and had been swallowed up by the earth (Numbers 16:32). The earth giving way is an apt analogy for the way it feels when everything is falling apart because we've taken on too much on our own, running our own lives. The thing about refuges is we have to run to them to find the shelter they offer (see Proverbs 18:10). That's why David writes again and again that he takes refuge in God (Psalms 7:1; 11:1; 16:1; 31:1; 57:1; 141:8; 143:9; 144:2). Each psalm is a prayer, and there are too many of them to miss. David is pointing to a way of understanding God that is vital to our relationship with Him and to the way we pray.

God is not only our place of refuge because He's the unassailable One who has existed before time and always will be; He's also our loving Father who speaks "tenderly" to us (Hosea 2:14). Moses uses both concepts in a single sentence, describing God as the One we run to and the One who carries us: "The eternal God is your refuge, and his everlasting arms are under you" (Deuteronomy 33:27 NLT). The peace God is able to give us is so strong and resilient that even the most heartrending situations cannot remove it from our lives.

April and Joseph are members of the church I serve. April attends our prayer meetings faithfully; Joseph joined our church a few years ago and resides in a state hospital. Years before I met them, April and Joseph were blessed with a baby girl, their only child. All seemed well, and they were happy together. But within a few years Joseph suffered from a sudden onset of mental illness. When their daughter was four years old, April came home from work one day to find their daughter's lifeless body. Joseph had killed her and fled but was apprehended at an airport.

Years later, April and Joseph remain married. When she became a member of our church, she met my wife and me for dinner and explained their situation, thinking we should be aware of it because of the news coverage their story had received. As Cari and I listened, we were amazed

Peace and Rest

by her faithfulness and comforted by God's ability to sustain her and Joseph together.

But that was only part of it. One evening, after working on this book that day, I pulled April aside after a prayer meeting and asked her, "How did you wrestle with God when you went through what you and Joseph suffered?"

April looked at me directly. "That's just the thing," she said with a wide-eyed smile, expressing her amazement. "I didn't."

My jaw dropped. "You didn't? How is that even possible?"

"This happened in January," she explained, "and a week before God had put a verse on my mind, and I felt like it was a gift from Him. It was Isaiah 26:3. ['You will keep in perfect peace those whose minds are steadfast, because they trust in you.'] I even told Joseph that I was looking forward to a year of peace and was excited about what it would bring. But what was happening was that God was preparing me, without my knowing it. James," she said intently, "*He carried me.* God carried me through that year, through all that time, and helped me trust Him when I couldn't see beyond my tears. This isn't about me at all," she said emphatically. "This is about the Lord. He got me through. He made it possible."

> **Life's crisis moments . . . often become wilderness places that God uses to bring us to a full stop, meet us afresh, and draw us closer to Himself.**

I didn't know what to say. I was taken aback by April's resolute faith and stunned by the God who made it all possible. She understood and smiled.

"Thank you for helping me remember." When I asked if she was sure it was OK that I shared their story, April responded again, "This isn't about me. This is all about God. He *carried* me."

Those words stuck in my head. Life's crisis moments—a sudden loss, a threatening illness, the sinful choices of a child or spouse—often become wilderness places that God uses to bring us to a full stop, meet us afresh, and draw us closer to Himself. Moses reminded God's people as they stood on the borders of the promised land that it was in the wilderness that "the LORD your God carried you, as a father carries his son, all the way you went until you reached this place" (Deuteronomy 1:31). God carries us more than we know. His Word reminds us that we "cannot keep [our]selves alive" (Psalm 22:29); every breath is a gift from Him. God holds us up through each moment of our lives, body and soul, "for in him we live and move and exist" (Acts 17:28 NLT).

Our challenge comes as we weigh God's goodness against the things that happen to us. If all is well, it's easier to believe that our Creator is kindly taking care of us. But in harder times when His goodness isn't as apparent, resting in Him can be tough. Without meaning to, our natural reaction can be to make ourselves (and the things that happen to us) the measure of all things, including the goodness of God.

Through His cross and resurrection, Jesus has triumphed over the brokenness of our world that came as a result of sin and has given us the "Good News of peace" (Ephesians 2:17 NLT). Shortly before He went to the cross, Jesus was very realistic with His followers about the fact that "in this world you will have trouble." Yet in the same breath He added, "But take heart! I have overcome the world" (John 16:33). His solution to the worst the world can throw at us isn't to dismiss our fears and worries as unrealistic or to give us "seven easy steps" to peace. His solution is to give us Himself.

If I didn't know April and Joseph and hadn't read the news reports, I might think their story was made up. I have chosen to change their names and keep them anonymous not at their request but because as their pastor I love them both and feel that they've suffered enough publicity. What is equally amazing to me is the way God has carried Joseph. I bring him Communion sometimes with elders from the church, and he helps lead a Bible study at the hospital. You would never know that he underwent the unthinkable years ago; God has done a healing work, sustained him in faith, and helped him to be an encouragement to others.

"He carried me." I can't get away from those words. They are an expression of praise from a thankful heart that demonstrates what our sovereign God is able to do and the depth of the peace He can give us in the most difficult seasons as we turn to Him. We may not have all the answers from God that we would like to have, but He is faithful still and has promised to be our refuge forever.

A Tender Rest

Yet another image Scripture uses multiple times to describe God as our protector is that of a mother bird with her young. Think of Jesus's words over Jerusalem shortly before His death: "How often I have longed to gather your children together, as a hen gathers her chicks under her wings, and you were not willing" (Matthew 23:37). It's a tender picture of closeness and protection, but once again it depends on the willingness of the one being sheltered. Psalm 91 begins, "Whoever dwells in the shelter of the Most High will rest in the shadow of the Almighty" (v. 1). "Hide me in the shadow of your wings," David prayed (17:8). "Because you are my help, I sing in the shadow of your wings. I cling to you" (63:7–8). David's words show the gentle sweetness of almighty God's loving rest for him.

How much more is God's rest available to us, knowing as we do that He loved us first "and sent his Son as a sacrifice to take away our sins" (1 John 4:10 NLT)? Resting through prayer helps us "remain" in Jesus's love (John 15:9) because it's easier to surrender our wills to Him when we're mindful that He's right there with us. To rest in Him is to "know and *rely* on the love God has for us" (1 John 4:16, emphasis added) and thus to intentionally live in His love as He carries us through life. Jesus announced that He came to proclaim "the Lord's favor" (Luke 4:19). Resting in Him is a way of consciously enjoying His favor throughout our lives.

This truth is beautifully expressed in the hymn "Jesus, I Am Resting, Resting," which is itself a prayer (and was the favorite hymn of Hudson Taylor during his impactful work as a missionary in China in the 1800s[2]):

> Ever lift Thy face upon me
> As I work and wait for Thee;
> Resting 'neath Thy smile, Lord Jesus,
> Earth's dark shadows flee.
> Brightness of my Father's glory,
> Sunshine of my Father's face,
> Keep me ever trusting, resting,
> Fill me with Thy grace.

Peace and Rest

The first photograph of a person was taken by Louis Daguerre in 1838. It shows a lone figure standing on an empty avenue in Paris during the middle of the day. Normally the streets and sidewalks would have been busy with activity, and in reality they were. But the people, horses, and carriages on the Boulevard du Temple that day were in constant motion, and the exposure time necessary to process the photo took seven minutes to capture the image. The lone man in the photograph was having his boots shined; he was the only person standing *still*.

With God, in a far more profound way, stillness accomplishes what constant motion and effort cannot. The stillness of our souls as we learn to rest in Him through prayer is something He blesses. "Be still, and know that I am God," He tells us (Psalm 46:10). The Hebrew word rendered "be still" is also sometimes translated as "cease striving." When we stop pushing, God meets us with His peace, and we find ourselves in the place where we were always meant to be.

PURSUING PEACE

- Think of a time in your life when God was carrying you. Bow your head and worship Him for His kindness.
- Take a moment to do nothing other than rest in Him, and ask Him to teach you how to rest in His care for you every day.
- Pray Ephesians 3:14–21 for someone you love. Consider asking someone to pray it with you for thirty days.

CHAPTER SIX

Peace in Low Places
Choosing Humility

Only he who is helpless can truly pray.
Ole Hallesby

Josh's life hadn't been easy, and the choices he'd made had caused himself and others pain. The tattoos on his face showed that. Three tattooed teardrops near his left eye and the numbers on his arms were telltale signs of a past in a gang and a stint behind bars.

But he was doing so much better now. When I met Josh, he was working in a secondhand store run by a rehab ministry in our city. In exchange for his efforts he was given a small stipend, meals, a roof over his head, and a new beginning. We struck up a conversation, and before we parted I asked him if there was anything I could pray for him about. "Just pray that I will be humble," he said. I promised him I would, but I walked away feeling convicted.

"Here I am," I thought, "asking how *I* can pray for *him*,

when it sounds like he should be praying for me. He's asking me to pray for something God absolutely loves, something wise and mature. When was the last time I asked God to help *me* be humble?"

It had been too long, and I thought about why. Part of it was because (I had to admit it) I'd been too busy and distracted lately, with my head filled with my life and my family and all the things I had to do. Another cause was that I'd fallen into the same kind of erroneous thinking you sometimes hear about praying for patience. "Never pray for patience," the reasoning goes. "If you do, God will allow some unfortunate series of events to occur that will force you to learn patience, and you really don't want that to happen." Of course Scripture doesn't say anything like that will happen, and it provides no examples of it happening in the lives of God's faithful people. But sometimes we allow our very human reasoning to keep us from asking for beautiful gifts God wants us to have.

It dawned on me that I had the same irrational fear about praying for humility—that God might then allow something to happen in my life that would humble me in a way I didn't like. Yet the opposite is actually true—Scripture provides myriad examples of people who never humbled themselves before God, and it didn't end well for them. (Just think of many of the kings of Israel and Judah and you get the idea.)

So before I reached the front of the store, I asked God to forgive me and prayed that He would help both Josh and me to be more humble. And I realized I had nothing to worry about in the asking. After all, aren't God's ways infinitely creative and wonderfully beyond our own? Jesus put it this way: "You fathers—if your children ask for a fish, do you give them a snake instead? Or if they ask for an egg, do you give them a scorpion? Of course not! So if you sinful people know how to give good gifts to your children, how much more will your heavenly Father give the Holy Spirit to those who ask him" (Luke 11:11–13 NLT).

The Bible indicates that humility is something God values deeply. And it's also something the devil pushes back against. In C. S. Lewis's brilliant book *The Screwtape Letters*, he imagines a conversation between a senior demon and his understudy, who is trying to tempt a young Christian, with this ironic twist:

> Your patient has become humble; have you drawn his attention to the fact? All virtues are less formidable to us once the man is aware that he has them, but this is specially true of humility. Catch him at the moment when he is really poor in spirit and smuggle into his mind the gratifying reflection, "By jove! I'm being humble," and almost immediately pride—pride at his own humility—will appear. If he awakes to the danger and tries to smother this new form of pride, make him proud of his attempt—and so on, through as many stages as you please. But don't try this too long, for fear you may awake his sense of humour and proportion, in which case he will merely laugh at you and go to bed.[1]

If you wonder about the influence humility can have on our prayers, there are few better examples than Moses. Numbers 12:3 tells us that "Moses was a very humble man, more humble than anyone else on the face of the earth." But Exodus 33:11 also explains that "the LORD would speak to Moses face to face, as one speaks to a friend." That doesn't establish a specific principle for our prayer lives ("Just be humble and you'll get to talk to God face-to-face like Moses did"), but it does give us a hint about God's heartfelt response to humility. God is drawn to people who aren't full of themselves. In fact, He promises to help and encourage those who want to turn from pride and self-will and draw near to Him. Thus He communicated through the prophet Isaiah:

> I live in a high and holy place,
> > *but also with the one who is contrite and*
> > > *lowly in spirit,*
> > to revive the spirit of the lowly
> > > and to revive the heart of the contrite.
> > > > (57:15, emphasis added)

A similar theme repeats throughout Scripture. Psalm 138:6 tells us that "though the LORD is great, he cares for the humble, but he keeps his distance from the proud" (NLT). In Zephaniah God tells His people, "I will remove all proud and arrogant people from among you. . . . Those who are left will be the lowly and humble" (3:11–12 NLT). He is so intent on communicating the importance of humility in His Word that the same verse appears three times: "God opposes the proud but shows favor to the humble" (James 4:6; 1 Peter 5:5; both are referencing Proverbs 3:34). Scripture cautions us over and over that God will oppose pride in our lives, at the same time making it clear that if we want to know His favor and His presence with us in an empowering way, we will make having humble hearts a personal goal.

Prayer can help us with this, though not the proud prayer of the Pharisee Jesus tells us about: "God, I thank you that I am not like other people . . ." (Luke 18:11). Jesus is clear that prayer like that doesn't get anywhere with God. Instead, He emphasizes that "all those who exalt themselves will be humbled, and those who humble themselves will be exalted" (v. 14). God gives His peace to those who learn how to set themselves aside and be humble before Him in prayer.

Pride or Presence?

The world we live in pushes back against humility. Our celebrity-fixated culture places an ever-increasing value on "being someone." If we don't take the time to sort things out carefully, we can find ourselves weighing our worth by the number of friends or followers we have on social media, thinking that the better known we are, the more we matter. But the God who chose the obscurity of a manger in Bethlehem over a cradle in a palace in Jerusalem sees things very differently.

There was a time in their lives when two of Jesus's disciples, James and John, wanted a special place of honor in His kingdom (so much that they had their mother ask for them). When the ten other disciples heard about it, Jesus called them together and told them, "Whoever wants to be a leader among you must be your servant" (Matthew 20:26 NLT). Heaven's value system flips earth's on its head; only those who learn to set themselves aside for God find themselves in a position to genuinely make a difference for Him in the world. It's not about the people we know or who know us. It goes much deeper.

A few years ago I encountered an older godly pastor and author who was a keynote speaker at a national conference.

There was nothing flashy about his presentation, but his ministry had reached many lives around the world as he did his best to communicate the truths of God's Word and to point others to Jesus. After the event was over, several of us were waiting outside the conference center for our rides. I noticed the pastor several yards away and walked over and told him how much I appreciated all he'd done.

Just at that moment his ride pulled up, and he smiled and nodded quickly and then turned his back to me to help his wife get into the car. I started walking back to wait for my own ride, thinking they had left, when there was a tap on my shoulder. It was the pastor, who had walked a good distance to catch me. "I'm sorry, I didn't mean to be abrupt," he said. "It's just that my wife isn't feeling well, and she needed to sit down; we had been waiting for our ride for almost an hour. Thank you so much for your encouragement. It means a great deal to me."

He didn't have to do that. He didn't know me; I was someone he'd only met moments before. His humility and empathy moved me, and I walked away with a new understanding of why his life and ministry had been impactful. His humble heart enabled me to catch a glimpse of the heart of Jesus. Just as early Christians had a term in Greek for Mary as the one who gave birth to Jesus (*Christotokos*, literally "Christ bearer"), this pastor clearly carried his Savior's presence within. Paul reminds us that the life and presence of Jesus dwells in all who have received Him: "We have this treasure in jars of clay" (2 Corinthians 4:7).

Because I'd followed this pastor's ministry for years, I knew spending time with God in prayer was deeply important to him. I saw for myself how this helped him stay grounded and demonstrate Christ's humility in a practical way.

Coming Down to Where Jesus Is

Right after Paul encouraged believers to "have the same attitude that Christ Jesus had" (Philippians 2:5 NLT), he points out that Jesus, who was

> in very nature God,
>   did not consider equality with God
>   something to be used to his own
>   advantage;
>   rather, he made himself nothing
>   by taking the very nature of a servant.
>   (vv. 6–7)

Think for a moment about how Jesus gave up every divine privilege out of love for us and our lost world. C. S. Lewis put the radical nature of Jesus's decision to become human in graphic terms: "The Eternal Being, who knows everything and who created the whole universe, became not only a man but (before that) a baby, and before that a *foetus* inside a Woman's body. If you want to get the hang of it, think how you would like to become a slug or a crab."² Given the lengths Jesus undertook to love us back to God—including going to the depths of such a cruel and publicly humiliating death on a cross—his life demonstrates an intentionally downwardly mobile path. And in this we again see His heart, the heart of the One who is "gentle and lowly" (Matthew 11:29 ESV). Following Him challenges us to move in the same heart-direction.

> **Think for a moment about how Jesus gave up every divine privilege out of love for us and our lost world.**

In a cringeworthy moment when the disciples were likely arguing *again* about which one of them would be the greatest in the kingdom of God, Jesus "called a little child to him, and placed the child among them" (Matthew 18:2). Then He said, "Unless you change and become like little children, you will never enter the kingdom of heaven" (v. 3).

Where is Jesus going with this? What does becoming like a little child have to do with entering the kingdom of God? Children usually aren't influencers in our world; that's left to celebrities and politicians and media moguls. But Jesus isn't about world influence. When the devil offered it to Him, Jesus rebuked him with the words of Deuteronomy 6:13: "Worship the Lord your God, and serve him only" (Matthew 4:10). Instead, Jesus calls us to be increasingly God- and kingdom-focused and promises that as we are, our heavenly Father will take care of our everyday needs (6:33).

> **Our heavenly Father lifts us up and pulls us close when we come to Him in prayer with simple, childlike faith.**

Children *have to* live humbly dependent lives, needing their parents or guardians to provide food and clothes and shelter. And Jesus likewise counterintuitively defines maturity in faith as a humble dependence on God, who was "pleased" to reveal the truths of His kingdom not to the "wise and learned" but to "little children" (11:25–26). Just as Jesus drew children near to pray for them and bless them when others saw little to be gained by their company (19:13), it's not a stretch to believe that our heavenly Father lifts us up and pulls us close when we come to Him in prayer with simple, childlike faith.

Peaceful Faith, Prayer Warriors, and Cub Scouts

But what is childlike faith? Tucked away in the three short verses of Psalm 131 is a fascinating description. It's a psalm Jesus no doubt knew well as one of the songs of ascents sung by the faithful on their way to the yearly religious festivals in Jerusalem, and we might wonder if He had it in mind when He said that we must become like children. David wrote,

> My heart is not proud, Lord,
>   my eyes are not haughty;
> I do not concern myself with great matters
>   or things too wonderful for me.
> But I have calmed and quieted myself,
>   I am like a weaned child with its mother;
>   like a weaned child I am content.
>
> Israel, put your hope in the Lord
>   both now and forevermore.

Some believe David wrote this prayer when he was young and being persecuted by King Saul. Others believe it may have been after his wife Michal scorned him for dancing before the Lord. While we may never know, what is clear is that David intentionally chooses to be humble. His description of a child that is no longer breastfeeding but is content simply to be in his mother's arms is also telling. David has decided to be content with God and is happy to be with Him, not demanding anything from Him. He is David's one great hope in all of life, and nothing matters more than living in an ongoing, prayerful relationship with the God of wonders under an open heaven.

Paul Miller expresses well both the challenge and the outcome of a life lived in such humble dependence: "What do I lose when I have a praying life? Control. Independence. What do I gain? Friendship with God. A quiet heart. The living work of God in the hearts of those I love. The ability to roll back the tide of evil. Essentially, I lose my kingdom and get his. I move from being an independent player to a dependent lover. I move from being an orphan to a child of God."[3] As we learn to quiet ourselves with the thought that Someone who loves us really does hold our lives in His hands and that He can be trusted regardless of what our feelings or experiences sometimes tell us, God comforts us and gives us fresh hope.

> We learn to accept our limits and let go of the need to have all the answers. . . . We instead learn to look expectantly to God, trusting His kindness.

In Psalm 131 David demonstrates what humbling ourselves looks and feels like. We learn to accept our limits and let go of the need to have all the answers or have things go exactly our way. We instead learn to look expectantly to God, trusting His kindness. We come to the happy realization that the term "prayer cub scout" fits us better than "prayer warrior," because we are always learning from God, and childlike faith is precious to Him (and as a result has great power). In exchange, we receive a growing awareness of God's love and a quiet understanding that Jesus is Immanuel, "God with us" (Matthew 1:23), and is actually present in our lives. With His presence comes an increase of His peace, the fruit of His Spirit at work within us (Galatians 5:22).

When childlike faith is ours, His peace can come inexplicably in the most unexpected circumstances, while it may evade those who are camped out on the question of why God allows certain things to happen. This is why the peace He gives "surpasses all understanding" (Philippians 4:7 ESV). Charles Spurgeon observed,

> The greatest blessing God gives is His presence. If I could choose any of life's blessings, I certainly would not ask for wealth, because wealth cannot bring freedom from pain, concern or anxiety. I certainly would not ask for popularity, because there is no rest for the world's leaders. My choice, my highest honor, would be to have God with me, always. When God is with us, there is no difference between Nebuchadnezzar's fiery furnace and a comfortable bed. It does not matter! We will be happy in either. If God is with us, if His divine love surrounds us, then we carry our own atmosphere and residence wherever we travel, and we can say with Moses, "Lord, you have been our dwelling place through all generations" (Psalm 90:1). The individual who can say this is full of heaven, full of God, and blessed beyond measure.[4]

Of course, Jesus is always present with those who have received Him; He promised He would be. But how can we live in such a way that we're increasingly aware of and humbly dependent on His presence with us? What might this look like for someone whose schedule is continually full or who struggles with chronic pain or health difficulties, or periodic anxiety or depression? To answer these questions, for the remainder of this chapter we'll take a closer look at prayer in the life of the man whose quote we just read, Charles Haddon Spurgeon.

Of Prophets in Rough Clothing and Pearls of Joy

Charles Spurgeon was arguably one of the most gifted and effective preachers in history, a silver-tongued orator sometimes referred to as "the prince of preachers." The church he pastored, the Metropolitan Tabernacle, located not far from the River Thames in South London, was the largest in the world at the time. Spurgeon's schedule was overwhelming: in addition to his voluminous writing and frequent preaching, under his careful leadership the church oversaw multiple endeavors, including orphanages, ministries to the poor and to women, and a pastor's college. (He was responsible for founding over sixty ministries in his lifetime.) Spurgeon was a juggernaut; it was not unusual for him to work eighteen-hour days.[5]

Spurgeon also suffered from numerous physical ailments, especially in his later years (he lived to age fifty-seven), including arthritis, debilitating gout that often caused his absence from the pulpit, and chronic nephritis, a painful inflammation of the kidneys. On top of all this, he sometimes battled depression, partly due to the withering criticisms he received as a result of his popular and uncompromisingly evangelical ministry, and partly because of his workload. Spurgeon felt that his struggles made him a more effective communicator of God's kindness to hurting people. In one autobiographical lecture to his ministry students, "The Minister's Fainting Fits," he wrote, "This depression comes over me whenever the Lord is preparing a larger blessing for my ministry; the cloud is black before it breaks."[6] He referred to depression as "a prophet in rough clothing, a John the Baptist, heralding the nearer coming" of God's rich goodness in a blessing that hadn't arrived yet but was about to.[7] Spurgeon learned to see even the hardships he faced as incidents that God used to draw him closer. Spurgeon was devoted, body and soul, to Jesus.

Hanging on the wall of my study is an original handwritten page from one of Spurgeon's sermons, which he edited with purple ink. (He used the color as a reminder of the believer's royal inheritance in Christ.) Spurgeon has fascinated me since my postgraduate studies, and I've since spent years delving into his passion for prayer. He edited this particular page after delivering a sermon on May 25, 1890. His message that day was entitled "Joy, Joy for Ever," and it emphasized the importance of simply loving God from the heart and staying before Him. It was drawn from Psalm 5:11:

> But let all who take refuge in you be glad;
>   let them ever sing for joy.
> Spread your protection over them,
>   that those who love your name may
>   rejoice in you.

Spurgeon maintained that what God has done for us in Jesus is so overwhelmingly good that we always have a reason to be joyful in Him:

> Our mirth is as soberly reasonable as the worldling's fears. Once more the happiness is a thing of the heart; for the text runs

thus—"Let them that *love thy name* be joyful in thee." We love God. I am speaking to many who could say, "Lord, thou knowest all things; thou knowest that I love thee." Is it not a very happy emotion? What is sweeter than to say, with the tears in one's eyes—"My God, I love thee!" To sit down and have nothing to ask for, no words to utter, but only for the soul to love—is this not heavenly? Measureless depths of unutterable love are in the soul, and in those depths we find the pearl of joy. When the heart is taken up with so delightful an object as the ever-blessed God, it feels an intensity of joy which cannot be rivaled.[8]

Like David, Spurgeon reminds us that this ongoing love relationship with our heavenly Father *is* prayer, where we draw strength, joy, and peace from daily taking comfort in His love for us. Prayer for Spurgeon is intensely practical, an everyday conversation with God with eternal impact. He credited the breathtaking success of his ministry to the prayers of others, continually encouraging them to pray. "What is to become of your minister . . . if you do not meet to pray for him?" he said on one occasion.[9]

What Spurgeon was after in his own life and the lives of those he served was intentional and spontaneous communication with Jesus about everything in life. Spurgeon encouraged spending one-on-one time with God both in the "morning and evening at the very least,"[10] cultivating an awareness of Jesus's presence with us throughout the day, and praying together regularly with others. His prayer recorded one Sunday morning sums up the heart-perspective behind this approach:

> Make every child of thine here to be every day serving Thee; and serving Thee so that heaven's work may begin below, and something of heavens' pleasure may be enjoyed even now. But Lord, while we work for Thee, always keep us sitting at the feet of Jesus. Let our faith never wander away from the simplicity of its confidence in Him. Let our motive never be anything but His glory; may our hearts be taken up with His love, and our thoughts perpetually engaged about His person. Let us choose the good part which shall not be taken away that if we serve with Martha we may also sit with Mary.[11]

Spurgeon's Preferred Way to Pray

Spurgeon's emphasis on "sitting at the feet of Jesus" in childlike confidence could sound like so much religious talk, but he meant it and taught passionately about how that kind of humble prayer was not only possible but could become a habit learned by anyone. Philip Yancey once commented that Jesus's teaching on prayer "reduces to three general principles: keep it honest, keep it simple, and keep it up."[12] Spurgeon encouraged short one-sentence prayers from the heart addressing God in any and every moment of life:

> You may be ... weighing your groceries, or you may be casting up an account, and

between the items you may say, "Lord, help me." You may breathe a prayer to heaven and say, "Lord, keep me." It will take no time. It is one great advantage to persons who are hard-pressed in business that such prayers as those will not, in the slightest degree, incapacitate them from attending to the business they may have in hand. . . . You can stand where you are, ride in a cab, walk along the streets. . . . No altar, no church, no so-called sacred place is needed, but wherever you are, just such a little prayer as that will reach the ear of God, and win a blessing. . . . On the land, or on the sea, in sickness or in health, amidst losses or gains, . . . still might he breathe his soul in short, quick sentences to God. The advantage of such a way of praying is that you can pray often and pray always . . . again and again and again—a hundred times a day. The habit of prayer is blessed, but the spirit of prayer is better.[13]

Spurgeon maintained that this spontaneous way of praying is the most natural way to pray and is "truly spiritual," because "wordy prayers may also be windy prayers."[14] Using Nehemiah's prayer before he answered King Artaxerxes's question (see Nehemiah 2:4) as an example, Spurgeon felt that quick prayers remind us of our need for God's help in everything. He felt too that "the habit of offering these brief prayers would also check your confidence in yourself. It would show your dependence upon God."[15] Noting that "God does not hear us because of the length of our prayer, but because of the sincerity of it,"[16] he suggested that prayer in every circumstance we face, whether temptation or exhaustion or pain, serves as a springboard into closeness with Him, opening the door to greater peace in His presence.

This childlike dependence at the heart of ongoing spontaneous prayer requires surrender. It's a kind of surrender that doesn't happen just once in our lives but continually throughout the day. It's the prayer of a heart that learns to say, "I'm yours, Lord," no matter what life may throw at us. The lower we bend in humility to Jesus, the more we discover that He has been there all along, and because He is, we are blessed. An old Puritan prayer sums up well the unexpected joy of this discovery:

> Let me learn by paradox
> that the way down is the way up,
> that to be low is to be high,
> that the broken heart is the healed heart,
> that the contrite spirit is the rejoicing spirit,
> that the repenting soul is the victorious
>   soul,
> that to have nothing is to possess all,
> that to bear the cross is to wear the crown,
> that to give is to receive,
> that the valley is the place of vision.[17]

PURSUING PEACE

- Read Psalm 131 and take some time to quiet yourself before God. Be still before Him, recognizing that the deepest need in your life is for Him.

- Is there a place in your life where you need to be more humble? Talk with Jesus about this, and ask for His help.
- Read the quote from Spurgeon about spontaneous praying again, and ask God to help you live in His peace by practicing this daily.

CHAPTER SEVEN

Hungering for Peace

Prayer from God's Word

> *Turn the Bible into prayer.*
> R. Murray M'Cheyne

"But God wants me to be happy!"

He was a handsome and successful man in the prime of life, with a beautiful wife and a career that took him to interesting places around the world. And he was having an affair.

We had been friends for some time and were out to lunch, and I'd just gently confronted him and told him that the road he was on wouldn't end well. He didn't want to hear it.

I pushed back against his pushing back. "Adultery, that's one of the big ten," I said, referring to the Ten Commandments. "Besides, didn't Jesus say it wouldn't always be easy? Didn't he say that if we want to follow Him, we'll have to deny ourselves and take up our cross?" I kept pressing carefully, mindful of the temptation he faced and how it was only God's grace to me that had kept me from going down the same path. "Hey, doesn't the Bible also say that anyone who wants to live a godly life will face persecution? Momentary happiness isn't always the only thing that matters."

He stood his ground. "I just think God wants me to be happy."

I was trying to be an actual friend, not someone who only told him what he wanted to hear. I tried to speak truth to him and turn him from the train wreck that inevitably would follow. But he wasn't buying it. He had turned from God's Word down a path that would lead to heartache. But characteristically, in the flush of an illicit romance, he didn't think it would. Though he was a believer in Jesus, Scripture had become something less than "the whole counsel of God"[1] and was now simply a book that he could pick and choose an occasional verse from to make him feel better. I hurt for him, and for his wife.

Paul instructed his young helper Timothy, "All Scripture is God-breathed and is useful for teaching, rebuking, correcting and training in righteousness, so that the servant of God may be thoroughly equipped for every good work" (2 Timothy 3:16–17). God breathes new life into us as we camp out in the pages of Scripture and weave it into the fabric of our lives. God's Spirit moves through His Word unlike any other place; it's not unusual to read the same passage for years, and suddenly God opens our eyes to a meaning we never knew was there. This is more than mere intellectual discovery; it's the leading of God's heart in our own as He calls us deeper into relationship and makes us more like Christ.

Help for Our Hearts

There is power in God's Word that can transform our thoughts and attitudes in a moment and give us hope and help we never had before. God's people have experienced this over and over again throughout history, and Scripture is filled with references about taking God's Word to heart (see Joshua 1:8; Psalms 1:2; 37:31; 40:8). Dietrich Bonhoeffer observed that the most promising way to pray "is to allow oneself to be guided by the word of the Scriptures, to pray on the basis of a word of Scripture. In this way we shall not become victims of our own emptiness."[2]

The Scriptures, especially the prayers of the Bible, help us learn to cry out to God from the heart by showing us how His people have prayed in life's many circumstances. They help us to be both bold and humble, and because they point us to God's character and attributes like his goodness and strength, they show us how to pray with faith.

> **The Scriptures, especially the prayers of the Bible, help us learn to cry out to God from the heart by showing us how His people have prayed in life's many circumstances.**

Think of the desperate way Jacob prayed before he faced his greatest fear in his brother, Esau, all the while reminding God of His promises to him: "I am unworthy of all the kindness and faithfulness you have shown your servant. . . . Save me, I pray, from the hand of my brother Esau, for I am afraid he will come and attack me. . . . But you have said, 'I will surely make you prosper and will make your descendants like the sand of the sea'" (Genesis 32:10–12). That short phrase "But you have said" sets a precedent for praying God's promises and His Word back to Him. If a human parent is moved by the plea, "But you promised!" how much more so is our Abba Father, who loves us profoundly more?

But the single best reason for learning to pray God's Word back to Him is that Jesus did it frequently, both singing and praying the Psalms. Matthew recalls that after Jesus and the disciples shared the Last Supper, "when they had sung a hymn, they went out to the Mount of Olives" (26:30). Because the Last Supper was a Passover meal, we know that according to tradition the final psalms of the Hallel (Psalms 113–118, which are songs of praise) were sung. When Jesus cried out, "My God, my God, why have you forsaken me?" (Matthew 27:46), He was praying the first verse of Psalm 22. His final words on the cross, "Into your hands I commit my spirit" (Luke 23:46), were a prayer from Psalm 31:5. The fact that Jesus prayed the words of Scripture in some of the most challenging moments of His life gives us a glimpse of how important this was to Him, and His command of Scripture's words even when undergoing extreme suffering and pain hints at his familiarity with it. His teaching that we do not live "on bread alone, but on every word that comes from the mouth of God" (Matthew 4:4) should also cause us to hunger for His Word as we pray.

Learning to pray God's Word guards us against emotional extremes, guiding our prayers with God's wisdom. Here Dietrich Bonhoeffer is helpful again. In his brief book *Psalms: The Prayer Book of the Bible*, he notes:

> Prayer does not mean simply to pour out one's heart. It means rather to find the way to God and to speak with him, whether the heart is full or empty. No one can do that on one's own. For that, one needs Christ. . . . Only in Jesus Christ are we able to pray, and with Him we also know that we shall

> be heard. . . . If we wish to pray with confidence and gladness, then the words of Holy Scripture will have to be the solid basis of our prayer. For here we know that Jesus Christ, the Word of God, teaches us to pray.[3]

Think of how Jesus's model prayer, the Lord's Prayer, shows us how to pray not just for the things we want and need ("Give us today our daily bread") but also for what God wants for us and for the world around us ("Your kingdom come, your will be done, on earth as it is in heaven") (Matthew 6:10–11). It's important to understand that the request for His kingdom—His leadership over the whole of our lives—comes before any other request for ourselves. It points us to a letting go of control, an accepting that everything isn't up to us. Jesus wants us to understand that something that seems so difficult—surrendering our needs and ourselves to God—is not only possible but desirable, because there's nowhere more restful than God's loving hands. As our lives are caught up in His love, we discover greater peace in Him.

The Message version of the Bible captures this thought well in the way it explains Jesus's teaching on the Lord's Prayer:

> The world is full of so-called prayer warriors who are prayer-ignorant. They're full of formulas and programs and advice, peddling techniques for what you want from God. Don't fall for that nonsense. This is your Father you are dealing with, and he knows better than you what you need. With

a God like this loving you, you can pray very simply. Like this:

Our Father in heaven,
Reveal who you are.
Set the world right;
Do what's best—
   as above, so below.
Keep us alive with three square meals.
Keep us forgiven with you and forgiving
   others.
Keep us safe from ourselves and the Devil.
You're in charge!
You can do anything you want!
You're ablaze in beauty!
   Yes. Yes. Yes. (vv. 7–13)

When we meet God prayerfully in His Word, He will meet us in our deepest places of need.

The Peace of Praying God's Word

A couple of years ago I was stricken with sudden nerve damage, which made walking excruciatingly painful. I was accustomed to being physically active and walking or running several miles a week, and all at once I had difficulty sitting or lying in bed. One day I was talking on the phone with my friend David Beaty, who has suffered from chronic pain for years. David is a pastor and author who has studied the prayer life of R. Murray M'Cheyne, a Scottish pastor from the early 1800s who encouraged his parishioners to "turn the Bible into prayer."[4]

Before our conversation concluded, David prayed for

me, recalling from memory several verses from a psalm. As I listened, it was as if David's voice wasn't the only voice I was hearing. I sensed God's Spirit moving through the words of Scripture, bringing new peace into a frustrating and painful place. While the physical pain continued for some time, I found I was better able to cope with it, more at peace with it. Much of the emotional burden I was carrying because of my condition lifted and didn't return.

The peace that comes as we place ourselves under God's Word is the result of His creative power and love, bringing strength and solutions we could never conceive of. Jesus is the Word through whom "all things were made" (John 1:3) and the "author of life" itself (Acts 3:15). He *is* life: "I am the way and the truth and the life. No one comes to the Father except through me," He reminds us (John 14:6). He is the Lord of life, and as His life fills our own through His Word, we are blessed to live for Him with new strength. Paul referred to this when he wrote about "all his [Christ's] energy that he powerfully works within me" (Colossians 1:29 ESV). The life He gives lasts forever and is our greatest need. Think of what Peter said to Jesus when others were walking away because He was saying things they didn't understand. When Jesus turned to the disciples and asked, "You do not want to leave too, do you?" Peter answered, "Lord, to whom shall we go? You have the words of eternal life" (John 6:67–68).

Just as the Spirit of God hovered over the waters when "the earth was without form and void" (Genesis 1:2 ESV), His Spirit moves in the empty places of our hearts to fill us with Himself and accomplish His creative and empowering purposes in our lives. Think of Jesus's winsome words, "I have come that [you] may have life, and have it to the full" (John 10:10). Each day He longs to pour more life into us. When we by faith welcome more of His Word into our hearts in the ways we think and pray, we will find Him in fresh ways. But we must seek *Him* and not just what He can do for us. We must seek His face and not just His hand.[5]

Praying the words of Scripture isn't some magic formula where if we say the right thing, God will answer us with the blessings we always wanted. That kind of thinking may sell a lot of books, but it ultimately doesn't draw us closer to Him because it places an emphasis on ourselves and leaves us disillusioned when our prayers don't seem to "work." But if we learn to read and pray Scripture because we are hungering for a deeper relationship with God, we will always find ourselves rewarded. As an aging King David told his son Solomon, "If you seek him, he will be found by you" (1 Chronicles 28:9).

> The best motives for learning to pray God's Word is love for Him and a desire to be closer.

Letting Peace In

The best motives for learning to pray God's Word is love for Him and a desire to be closer, because we understand that He loved us first (1 John 4:19) and wants us to be with Him always. The same Jesus who healed the sick and calmed the storms in nature and in the hearts of hurting people is near us and for us. He wants to help us live in His peace more and more, thus Scripture reminds us, "*Let* the peace of Christ rule in your hearts" (Colossians 3:15, emphasis added).

Notice that the language Scripture uses here describes something we have to allow to happen, even though it's grammatically a command, and the original language implies action that is continuous. In other words, "Keep letting it happen!" God's peace is more than able to rule in our hearts, but we have to make a practice of choosing to let it in, to let *Him* in, because "The Lord Is Peace" (Judges 6:24). This is also how we are to "be transformed by the renewing" of our minds (Romans 12:2). We don't transform ourselves. We are once again on the receiving end of what God does; God changes us as we place ourselves prayerfully before Him in His Word. Think of turning on a faucet: you don't make the water flow; you let it in. There's a flow to God's peace, and the language Scripture uses to describe it is perpetual. God promises to extend peace to His people "like a river" (Isaiah 66:12). God's peace, like flowing water, has a force and movement all its own, empowered by His Spirit.

So how can we open the floodgates? God's Word provides an indispensable key for discovering more of His peace in our daily lives. "Those who love your instructions have great peace and do not stumble," one of the psalmists discovered (Psalm 119:165 NLT). The connection between living close to God through His Word and having His peace within us is promised in God's Word, and it's one of the reasons why we need to take Scripture to heart daily. Reading and praying Scripture helps us listen to God and interact with Him, letting more of His life-giving presence flow in. This is more than simply an experience; sometimes we're aware of God's Spirit at work within us, while other times we may not realize it until hours later. It's the outworking of Jesus's loving friendship within us. As R. Murray M'Cheyne explained,

> What an intimate friendship this is! Can any friendship be compared with this? Another friend may dwell in our neighborhood; he may dwell in our family; but, ah! here is

a friend that dwells in us. Can there be a greater friendship than this? When the Lord Jesus came from heaven and dwelt among us—when He dwelt with Martha and Mary, and Lazarus . . . that was friendship. But it was still greater friendship for the Holy Spirit to come and dwell in a clay cottage . . . and this is the friendship of the Holy Spirit to a believing soul.[6]

Several years ago I was going through one of the most difficult times of my life when I was gravely misunderstood by others I loved and was doing my best to serve. The situation and personalities involved were accusatory and unrelenting, and as every attempt at reconciliation failed, depression descended on me like a dark cloud. This was a spiritual attack I hadn't seen coming. (We'll address the topic of spiritual oppression in the next chapter.) I couldn't see through my discouragement enough to hope for any kindness that was about to come my way. All I could do was cling to God, placing myself under His Word daily. (The word "under" is carefully chosen here—it's one thing to be *in* God's Word but another to submit ourselves to God's Spirit as we read it.)

Years before I had developed the habit of reading through the Bible every year, and one morning I was sitting at the kitchen table reading and praying. I felt deeply wounded; there was so much I didn't understand, including why God had allowed the painful events to happen. Reading wasn't easy. It was as if all I could do was crawl into the pages of God's Word, placing myself before Him. But that morning, my eyes fell upon a verse, and it was as if a light beamed from the pages and penetrated my soul. In an instant, all of the past hurts fell into perspective, much of the pain vanished, and I was able to hope again in a lasting, substantive way. My sadness lifted, as if Jesus Himself had come and sat down at the table beside me, speaking His healing truth tenderly to me and giving me everything I needed. What the verse was I'll keep between me and God so as not to distract from what His Spirit did with it, but suffice it to say that I wouldn't trade those moments before Him for anything.

As you read your Bible, ask God to speak to you and to help you be sensitive to His Spirit about anything He wants to communicate. Then as you encounter His Word, pray it back to Him, asking any questions you may have and sharing any observations about your life. Remember that God isn't impressed with our ability to quote Scripture when we pray; we don't have to be discouraged if we have difficulty memorizing verses. Sometimes just praying a few words that God brings to our attention when we're reading is a very effective way to begin a heart-to-heart with our heavenly Father. Because "the word of God is alive and active" (Hebrews 4:12), this is never dull; it's a vital way of interacting with Him and keeping our relationship with Him before us as we go through the day. Just a few words from God's Word, applied to our hearts by His Spirit at the right moment, can transform our lives.

When I was twenty, I was pushing hard against what I was fearful might be God's call into pastoral ministry. Because I love languages, I was intent on pursuing what I planned to be a lucrative career in international business. But even though things looked promising and the right grad school was opening up, I had no peace about it. So I asked the counsel of a friend.

George was a genuinely humble man whose love for Jesus was evident. He was a janitor in the library at my school and also pastored a Black church in the city. After he listened intently to my interior battle, he gave me a knowing glance. "You know, when Jesus had a decision to make, He fasted. Have you ever tried that?" I had never fasted before in my life, but the next Saturday I decided to give it a try.

I spent the day in my dorm room, drinking only water and prayerfully reading my Bible. But by the end of the afternoon, I had nothing. Then I remembered my mother often pointed me toward the epistle of James, so I started in on it. When I got to the fourth chapter, these words came alive with meaning: "Now listen, you who say, 'Today or tomorrow we will go to this or that city, spend a year there, carry on business and make money.' Why, you do not even know what will happen tomorrow. What is your life? You are a mist that appears for a little while and then vanishes. Instead, you ought to say, 'If it is the Lord's will, we will live and do this or that'" (vv. 13–15).

My answer was clear, and I stopped running from what I believed was the direction God wanted for my life. I even started looking forward to it. When we follow Jesus's example by praying Scripture, even a few words can change our outlook and help us draw closer to Him. There are

> **When we follow Jesus's example by praying Scripture, even a few words can change our outlook and help us draw closer to Him.**

prayers, promises, and assurances in the Bible that we don't want to live without. His peace is always available to us, and as we consistently place ourselves under His Word, we take steps into a place where we can encounter it more and more. For those of us who have received Christ, God has already made peace with us "through his blood, shed on the cross" (Colossians 1:20). He welcomes us to walk into this peace, and His Word is "a lamp" for our feet and "a light" for our "path" (Psalm 119:105).

For the next few pages, we'll look at several scriptural prayers and promises that we can turn into prayer to help us live into the peace God longs for us to have. Beside each of the Scriptures, a few brief "prayer starters" have been added to help you pray. These are prayers you can pray over and over again and make your own. They cover several different aspects of our relationship with God that are important for peace with Him, including praising Him for His faithfulness, humbling ourselves before Him, asking for His peace, and trusting Him with the present and the future.[7] This list is anything but comprehensive; you may think of several other verses to pray as you read through them, and I hope you will! Praying God's Word is a lifelong adventure—an adventure that we take with Him—and places that are breathtaking in beauty and meaning await us as we choose to follow Him there.

Walking into Peace through Praying God's Word

Loving God with Praise

Praising God helps us realize His greatness; it takes our eyes off ourselves and our circumstances and lifts them to the One who deeply cares for us and is over all.

> I will praise you், Lᴏʀᴅ, with all my heart;
> I will tell of all the marvelous things you have done.
> I will be filled with joy because of you.
> (Psalm 9:1–2 ɴʟᴛ)

Notice the intentionality here: "I will" is repeated three times. Add your own "I will" as you pray it. For example, "I will rest in your love today."

> I love you, Lᴏʀᴅ; you are my strength.
> (Psalm 18:1 ɴʟᴛ)

Tell God why you love Him, and ask Him with faith for the strength He gives.

> Oh, how my soul praises the Lord.
> How my spirit rejoices in God my Savior! . . .
> For the Mighty One is holy,
> and he has done great things for me.
> (Luke 1:46–47, 49 ɴʟᴛ)

What great things has God done for you? Name some of them before Him and praise Him for them.

> Praise the Lord, praise God our savior!
> For each day he carries us in his arms.
> (Psalm 68:19 ɴʟᴛ)

Rest in His love for you as you pray, "Each day you carry me in your arms," and lift your heart to Him in love.

> All praise to God, the Father of our Lord Jesus Christ. God is our merciful Father and the source of all comfort. He comforts us in all our troubles so that we can comfort others. (2 Corinthians 1:3–4 NLT)

Praise God for the mercies you've seen in your life, and because His comfort isn't meant to be kept to ourselves, ask that He will help you to share His comfort with others.

> He has rescued us from the dominion of darkness and brought us into the kingdom of the Son he loves. (Colossians 1:13)

Thank Jesus that He has rescued you and that you live in the spiritual reality of His kingdom, where His peace can be increasingly present in your life.

Humbling Ourselves

Humbling ourselves isn't about tearing ourselves down. It's about magnifying God (emphasizing His greatness) and recognizing our need for Him in everything. When we humble ourselves, we place ourselves before God as His servants, but we are also His friends. Because He has rescued us entirely through the goodness of His love, we want to be sensitive to anything that could cause distance in our relationship and openly bring it before Him.

> O Sovereign LORD, you have only begun to show your greatness and the strength of your hand to me, your servant. (Deuteronomy 3:24 NLT)

Thank God for His kindness to you and for all that you have to look forward to in Him.

> Yet you, LORD, are our Father.
> We are the clay, you are the potter;
> we are all the work of your hand.
> (Isaiah 64:8)

Thank God for giving you life and calling you to Him in love.

> Create in me a clean heart, O God.
> Renew a loyal spirit within me.
> (Psalm 51:10 NLT)

Talk to God about any sins you are struggling with, and ask for forgiveness and a loyal heart. Receive the gift of His forgiveness by faith, and thank Jesus for giving Himself so that you can live at peace with God (2 Corinthians 5:19).

> People do not live by bread alone, but by every word that comes from the mouth of God. (Matthew 4:4 NLT)

Ask God to help you to love His Word and to hunger for it daily, because those who love God's Word "have great peace" (Psalm 119:165 NLT).

> I have come that they may have life, and have it to the full. (John 10:10)

Sit quietly before Jesus and ask Him to fill you with the life and peace that only comes from Him.

Asking for Peace

> Peace I leave with you; my peace I give you. I do not give to you as the world gives. Do not let your hearts be troubled and do not be afraid. (John 14:27)

As you read these words, imagine that Jesus is saying them directly to you (because He actually is), giving you peace as His gift. Then tell Him, "Yes, Lord. I receive your peace!"

> He leads me beside quiet waters,
>   he refreshes my soul.
>   (Psalm 23:2–3)

Thank Jesus that He is your Shepherd, and ask Him to refresh your soul with His presence, love, and peace.

> You will keep in perfect peace
>   all who trust in you,
>   all whose thoughts are fixed on you!
>   (Isaiah 26:3 NLT)

Ask God to help you trust Him and to keep your heart and mind increasingly at rest in Him.

> Now may the Lord of peace himself give you peace at all times and in every way. (2 Thessalonians 3:16 ESV)

Thank Jesus that His peace is always available to you because He is always available! Thank Him for being near, no matter what you may face.

> May God give you more and more grace
> and peace as you grow in your knowledge
> of God and Jesus our Lord. (2 Peter 1:2 NLT)

This prayer, like the one above, is a blessing prayer. Make it personal by addressing God directly, changing the pronouns from "you" and "your" to "me," "I," and "my."

Trusting God with Our Present and Future

> Those who know your name trust in you,
>   for you, O Lord, do not abandon those
>   who search for you.
> (Psalm 9:10 NLT)

Praise God that He, your Peace, will always be right there for you, and that He has promised to never leave you or abandon you (Hebrews 13:5).

> Let the peace that comes from Christ rule in
> your hearts. (Colossians 3:15 NLT)

Ask for His peace to fill your heart and mind. Place any worry or fear that you have before Jesus, and ask Him to replace it with His peace.

> The mind governed by the Spirit is life and
> peace. (Romans 8:6)

Ask God to help you yield to His Spirit and trust Him in every area of your life, so that you are increasingly filled with His peace.

> Let me hear of your unfailing love each
>   morning,

> for I am trusting you.
> Show me where to walk,
> for I give myself to you.
> (Psalm 143:8 NLT)

Pray this prayer to start your day, and ask God to help you to keep His love and peace before you in everything you do.

> In peace I will lie down and sleep,
> for you alone, LORD,
> make me dwell in safety.
> (Psalm 4:8)

A great prayer for laying down our worries before we go to bed! Thank God for always watching over you, and rest in His loving care for you.

PURSUING PEACE

- Choose several verses from the "Walking into Peace through Praying God's Word" section of this chapter and pray them, asking Jesus to fill you with His peace.
- Thank God for speaking to us through His Word, and ask Him to help you listen attentively as you read it.
- What is your favorite Scripture verse to pray from memory? Tell God why you love it, and worship Him for it.

CHAPTER EIGHT

Fighting for Peace
Armored for Prayer

*The whole meaning of putting on the
armor of God is about prayer.*

Oswald Chambers

It was a small space to fit into, even for a skinny nine-year-old. The earthen ceiling and floor of the cave opened out into a larger limestone cavern, but you had to crawl through the narrow space to make it in. I had made it in without a problem. I didn't realize that making it out would be more difficult.

I had tagged along with my brothers and an older friend, spelunking in an uncharted natural cave not far from our home. Of course, none of us had asked our parents for permission; we all knew they wouldn't let us do it, which made the adventure all the more alluring. Fortunately, our guide, a "trail-wise" adventurer of the mature age of thirteen, had been there before and knew better than to go too far in, but it was in my hurry to get out that it happened. I got stuck. The ceiling of the cave seemed to close in on

Peace through Prayer

me like a vise. My brothers were reaching out their hands to me, coaxing me to pull myself out. But my body was tense and I was starting to panic. What was mere minutes seemed like an eternity; I thought I'd be stuck there forever. Finally, the older boy came back into the space and told me I could make it. He talked to me and helped me to calm down. Then he took my hand and pulled me out.

As the years went by, I forgot about that incident. Maybe I blocked it out, shelving it somewhere under the category of things I did as a kid that I'd rather not talk to my guardian angel about someday. But one day it came back; I woke up in the middle of the night, remembering. Suddenly it was all there—the growing fear bordering on panic, that feeling of being trapped with nothing but a wall above me. It came back not just one night but every night, whenever I awakened. But now it was different. This time it was dark, there was no light at all, and I was entirely alone.

After several nights of this, I began to understand what was happening. This was more than just a memory. This was a bad memory that had been taken and twisted to make it even worse. This was a spiritual attack.

The realization was a relief. Now I knew how to fight it. Just as every attack in battle has a defense or countermove, so did this one. Every night that it happened, I began to pray. I prayed before I went to bed, asking God to take away my fear. I prayed the instant the thoughts came closing in, calling on Jesus and acknowledging that He was with me. I repeated His words in my mind: "Peace I leave with you; my peace I give you. I do not give to you as the world gives. Do not let your hearts be troubled and do not be afraid" (John 14:27). I prayed my way through the Twenty-Third Psalm, pausing at the words where the psalm first becomes a prayer: "Even though I walk through the valley of the shadow of death, I will fear no evil, for *you* are with me" (v. 4 ESV, emphasis added).

As quickly as the attacks came, the darkness retreated. I was surprised at how suddenly it happened. Like pests that scatter when you turn on a light, the twisted memories ceased after only a few nights of praying that way, and God had done a healing work in my heart and mind.

Panic attacks are a common experience for many. Not all panic attacks are spiritual in nature, but God has given us prayer as a powerful help and remedy whenever our adversary, the devil, comes against us. As we saw in the previous chapter, the peace God desires for us isn't simply something we passively receive. Sometimes it's something we have to fight for, not because God doesn't want us to have it but because we live in a fallen world where our "adversary the devil prowls around like a roaring lion, seeking someone to devour" (1 Peter 5:8 ESV). Scripture's advice on how to handle this is also clear: "Resist him, standing firm in the faith" (v. 9). This advice can only point us to prayer and God's Word. How else could we find the strength to overcome such singular evil? We must stand in the strength God gives and not our own. There is peace in His strength.

The Gap in Our Armor

Paul's famous passage in Ephesians 6 on the full armor of God is a favorite for many believers. When Paul first introduces the concept, he reminds his readers that "we are not fighting against flesh-and-blood enemies, but against evil rulers and authorities of the unseen world, against mighty powers in this dark world, and against evil spirits in the heavenly places" (v. 12 NLT). The description of the armor that immediately follows is to prepare us so that after we "have done everything," we may be able "to stand" against forces where we would otherwise be outmatched (v. 13).

Do a search online for "the armor of God" and multiple images will come up of someone clad in Roman armor, with the individual pieces identified and their spiritual significance listed beside each one. There's "the belt of truth" and "the breastplate of righteousness," "feet fitted with the readiness that comes from the gospel of peace," "the shield of faith," "the helmet of salvation," and "the sword of the Spirit, which is the word of God" (vv. 14–17). Many of the illustrations online are of course biblical, helpful, and encouraging, but nine out of ten times there's a problem with them. They're incomplete.

It helps to understand that the original language of the New Testament (Koine Greek) was written without paragraph breaks. Because we use them in English, they had to be inserted in our translations. Whenever we see a paragraph break, we automatically assume that a new topic is beginning after the previous one has concluded. But sometimes a paragraph break has been inserted in the English before a topic has finished, and this is the case between Ephesians 6:17 and 18 in many translations. This matters significantly because the explanation of the purpose of the full armor of God in our lives isn't found until you read the verses of the paragraph that follows: "And pray in the Spirit on all occasion with all kinds of prayers and requests. With this in mind, be alert and always keep on praying for all the Lord's people. Pray also for me, that whenever I speak, words may be given me so that I will fearlessly make known the mystery of the gospel, for which I am an ambassador in chains. Pray that I may declare it fearlessly, as I should" (vv. 18–20).

If we leave those verses out, we might be tempted to think that Paul is being poetic or metaphorical, writing in a descriptive way without really telling us *how* to practically apply the different elements of the armor of God to our lives. But Paul is actually drawing on an earlier Old Testament passage that describes God coming to rescue His people: "He put on righteousness as his breastplate, and the helmet of salvation on his head" (Isaiah 59:17). So Paul's starting point isn't an emphasis on ourselves but on God and how we are to turn to Him. The armor is His, as is the strength we need. And there's only one way to get it.

Go over Ephesians 6 again starting with verse 10, reading into the next paragraph, and don't stop until you get to verse 20. In those final three short verses you'll see one thought repeated over and over. There are six words that point to the real purpose of the armor of God: "pray," "prayers," "requests," "praying," "pray," "pray" (vv. 18–20). Notice also the breadth with which these words are applied. We are to pray "on *all* occasions with *all* kinds of prayers and requests," staying aware so that we "*always* keep on praying for *all*" God's people (v. 18, emphasis added). These four "alls" describe a life that is devoted to prayer and raise important questions. Have we been trying to apply the pieces of the armor of God to our lives without realizing what they're actually for? If the real purpose of the armor of God is to protect us when we pray, won't our praying be helped if we make it a greater priority?

All-Prayer: Running to Strength

Previous generations of believers understood the concept of "all-prayer" better than our own. In his inimitable way,

Charles Spurgeon described all-prayer as an unfailing strategy for any believer who is faced with spiritual attack:

> When you cannot use your sword you may take to the weapon of all-prayer. Your powder may be damp, your bow-string may be relaxed, but the weapon of all-prayer need never be out of order. Leviathan laughs at the javelin, but he trembles at prayer. Sword and spear need furbishing, but prayer never rusts, and when we think it most blunt it cuts the best. Prayer is an open door which none can shut. Devils may surround you on all sides, but the way upward is always open, and as long as that road is unobstructed, you will not fall into the enemy's hand.[1]

God uses our prayers to protect us from enemy attacks on our peace and joy in Jesus. We can pray in any moment, even when we may not have the opportunity to read God's Word ("the sword of the Spirit"). Prayer is available when everything around us seems hopeless. There's so much power in it that it puts our enemy on the defensive.

A generation before Spurgeon, William Cowper summed up the relationship between the power of prayer and the armor of God this way:

> Restraining prayer, we cease to fight:
> Prayer makes the Christian's armour
>   bright:
> And Satan trembles when he sees
> The weakest saint upon his knees.[2]

The devil trembles when we pray not because of any strength we have but because of the infinite, all-powerful Father whom we call on, whose "power is made perfect in weakness" (2 Corinthians 12:9).

In the award-winning French animal adventure film *The Bear*, there's a gripping scene where an orphaned grizzly cub is hunted and pursued by a large mountain lion. The cub does his best to run away, but the stronger and faster lion gains ground. The cub tries to flee across a river but is cornered, and with the swipe of a paw the lion bloodies his mouth. At this point the only thing the poor cub can do is stand his ground. He crouches on his back legs and growls. At first the noise he makes sounds like a pitiful whine, but then the growl that seems to come from him is far more menacing than he's capable of. The lion lowers his ears and cowers back, retreating just as the camera angle swings around to reveal a nine-foot-tall male Kodiak bear standing directly behind the cub, protecting him with a mighty roar.

The scene is an unintentional but apt depiction of scriptural truth. We can't prevail against the "roaring lion" who is our adversary in our own strength, thus "the weapons we fight with are not the weapons of the world" (2 Corinthians 10:4). Oswald Chambers explains succinctly, "The armor is for the battle of prayer. . . . The armor is not to fight in, but to shield us while we pray. Prayer is the battle."[3] The point is that God is inviting us

> **God is inviting us into a place of His strength through prayerful dependence on Him, so that we may live with hope and peace when confronted with the evils we inevitably face.**

into a place of His strength through prayerful dependence on Him, so that we may live with hope and peace when confronted with the evils we inevitably face. But faithful prayer requires effort. We come up against distractions and discouragement and the plotting of an adversary who wants us to do anything but run to God, knowing that if we make a habit of doing so, we will find Him to be our "fortress" and our "deliverer" (Psalm 18:2). We will "be strong in the Lord and in his mighty power" (Ephesians 6:10).

Putting on Armor for Prayer

Discovering that the armor of God is intended to help us when we pray may be a slightly different perspective than we're used to. But as Andrew Bonar observed, "Satan has a special ill-will to praying people. Someone has said that Satan's orders are . . . 'Fight not with that saint nor that other, but only with the praying people.'"[4] Once the concepts Paul describes as armor are applied to the way we pray, they take on new meaning. So because we are to "put on the full armor" (Ephesians 6:11), let's look at each piece individually and how they help us when we pray.

The Belt of Truth

First, "the belt of truth buckled around your waist" (Ephesians 6:14) describes the new spiritual reality we live in when we come to Christ. Paul explains this just two chapters earlier in Ephesians, where he contrasts those who "are darkened in their understanding and separated from the life of God" because of "the hardening of their hearts" with those who live changed lives through "the *truth* that is in Jesus" (4:18, 21, emphasis added). Because of the truth that comes from Jesus, you and I can "let the Spirit renew [our] thoughts and attitudes" and "put on [our] new nature" in Him (vv. 23–24 NLT).

This new nature means that we can truly have hope when we pray because we are now God's children and He is our faithful Father. He is with us and for us. Entirely because of His goodness to us, we're different since He's saved us, and the new identity He has given us transforms who we were, who we are, and who we are becoming. As we come to Him, we can be truthful about our sins and struggles, understanding that we are deeply loved, and because we are, real spiritual growth is truly possible. We can be genuine with Him, knowing that He hears our prayers with a willing and responsive heart. We put on the belt of truth in prayer when we understand that what Jesus has done for us shields and protects us at the very core of who we are.

The Breastplate of Righteousness

The second part of the armor is the "breastplate of righteousness." It isn't our own righteousness we put on but Christ's. "He saved us, not because of works done by us in righteousness, but according to his own mercy, by the washing of regeneration and renewal of the Holy Spirit" (Titus 3:5 ESV).

Our sins and weaknesses are evident to us on so many levels, but Jesus has rescued us. Because He "is at the right hand of God and is also interceding for us" (Romans 8:34), we can "come boldly to the throne of our gracious God," receiving His mercy and finding "grace to help us when we need it most" (Hebrews 4:16 NLT). His righteousness (or "right living") on our behalf is the very opposite of self-righteousness, because He has done it all for us: "Christ made us right with God; he made us pure and holy, and he freed us from sin" (1 Corinthians 1:30 NLT). His goodness to us compels us to want to live better lives, because we long to be close to Him and understand that when we cherish sin in our hearts, it grieves God's Spirit and negatively impacts our prayers (see Psalm 66:18). To put on the breastplate of righteousness when we pray means to agree with God about the things He desires for our life and the world and to go after them with our prayers, to "seek first his kingdom and his righteousness" (Matthew 6:33).

Fitted Feet

The third part of the armor is vital for being able to *stand*, something Paul underscores four times in Ephesians 6. "For shoes, put on the peace that comes from the Good News so that you will be fully prepared" (v. 15 NLT). As with the other parts of the armor, we are only able to stand in God's strength and not our own. But because of His strength, we *can* stand "against the devil's schemes" (v. 11). We can pray with confidence, knowing that our prayers are precious to God. Even when we feel defeated, we can take heart and continue to pray, knowing that the One who is in us "is greater than the one who is in the world" (1 John 4:4).

The peace Jesus offers is available to us, waiting, but it's something we have to choose to put ourselves into. The shoes Paul had in mind were those worn by Roman infantry, which had metal spikes or cleats enabling soldiers to dig in and hold their ground against their enemies. In Revelation, John refers to the devil as "the accuser of our brothers and sisters, who accuses them before our God day and night" (12:10). His attacks on us when we pray can be withering: "Do you think God will hear *your* prayers after the things you've done? Do you honestly believe God could forgive you and call you His own?" Our defense is the peace of the good news, that we "who once were far off have been brought near by the blood of Christ" (Ephesians 2:13 ESV).

When we pray, we take our stand in all that Jesus is, accepting the truth that we are completely forgiven and "have peace with God because of what Jesus" has done for us (Romans 5:1 NLT). His peace isn't dependent on what others say or think about us; it's ours through His unconditional love for us, received by faith. As we stand on His merits each day and live in love with Him, our accuser's attacks on who we are become less frequent, so that "the God of peace will soon crush Satan under your feet" (16:20).

The good news of all that Jesus is goes so deep that it can even transform our relationships. Paul points to this in Ephesians 2, when he talks about the hatred between Jews and Gentiles and then says of Jesus that "he himself is our peace, who has made the two groups one and has destroyed the barrier, the dividing wall of hostility" (v. 14). Letting God's peace into our inmost thoughts about our relationships is indispensable for prayer. Bitterness and a lack of forgiveness impede our praying because we ourselves stand so deeply in need of His mercy. Think of Jesus's parable of the unmerciful servant, a man who had been forgiven much but still could not forgive. Jesus concludes by urging us in the strongest of terms to "forgive your brother or sister from your heart" (Matthew 18:35). If we fail to do this, we make ourselves vulnerable to the enemy's attack. The writer of Hebrews underscores this warning: "Watch out that no poisonous root of bitterness grows up to trouble you, corrupting many" (12:15 NLT).

The peace Jesus gives us is to overflow in our hearts and lives into the lives of others. Even when others have deeply wronged us, as we pray, God is able to give us more of Himself and help us to forgive—even when part of us doesn't want to.

In her book *The Hiding Place*, Dutch author Corrie ten Boom tells about encountering a former Nazi SS guard for the first time since she had seen him at the Ravensbrück prison camp, the same camp where her sister perished. The guard had been posted outside the showers in the processing center where prisoners entered the camp, which was humiliating for the women there. But now years later, the man had become a sincere believer. Corrie was speaking at a church, and afterward the former guard approached her. Suddenly harsh memories from the past rushed in and gripped her like a vise:

> He came up to me as the church was emptying, beaming and bowing. "How grateful I am for your message, Fraulein," he said. "To think that, as you say, He has washed my sins away!"
>
> His hand was thrust out to shake mine. And I, who had preached so often to the people in Bloemendaal the need to forgive, kept my hand at my side.
>
> Even as the angry, vengeful thoughts boiled through me, I saw the sin of them. Jesus Christ had died for this man; was I

going to ask for more? "Lord Jesus," I prayed, "forgive me and help me to forgive him." I tried to smile, I struggled to raise my hand. I could not. I felt nothing, not the slightest spark of warmth or charity. And so again I breathed a silent prayer. "Jesus," I prayed, "I cannot forgive him. Give me Your forgiveness."

As I took his hand the most incredible thing happened. From my shoulder along my arm and through my hand a current seemed to pass from me to him, while into my heart sprang a love for this stranger that almost overwhelmed me.

And so I discovered that it is not on our forgiveness any more than on our goodness that the world's healing hinges, but on His. When He tells us to love our enemies, He gives, along with the command, the love itself.[5]

The forgiveness Jesus works in us may not always happen so quickly or dramatically. We may have to pray again and again. But if we are sincerely seeking Him, the Holy Spirit will convict us of our need to be consistent and to take our stand on all that He has done for us. This will always point us to greater dependence on Him in prayer and will compel us to forgive and to live at peace with others, whom Jesus also loves and died to save. This forgiveness can happen even if another hasn't repented or asked for forgiveness, because it's made possible through the One who said, "Father, forgive them, for they know not what they do" (Luke 23:34 ESV).

In the Sermon on the Mount, Jesus encouraged us with the words, "Blessed are the peacemakers, for they will be called children of God" (Matthew 5:9). The word for "blessed" in the original language of that verse may also be translated "happy" or "fortunate." As we resist the enemy's temptations to hate and ungodly attitudes of division and we step closer to our Savior, His love flows in, and our happiness increases. The world around us may be continually caught up in the misery of divisiveness and contention, but God's Word encourages us, "If it is possible, as far as it depends on you, live at peace with everyone" (Romans 12:18).

> **As we resist the enemy's temptations to hate and ungodly attitudes of division and we step closer to our Savior, His love flows in.**

Shielded by Faith

The fourth piece of the armor for prayer is "the shield of faith" (Ephesians 6:16). Roman shields were often made of wood and leather, which could be soaked with water to put out flaming arrows. In chapter 4 we looked at how even a little faith, placed in God's hands, is a powerful thing when we pray. Here, Scripture points to how necessary faith is for overcoming Satan's attacks. As before, it's faith not in ourselves or our ability to believe but in the conquering "Lion of the tribe of Judah" (Revelation 5:5). "Through faith" in Him we "are shielded by God's power" (1 Peter 1:5).

This is faith that helps us when we pray. As Paul writes, "Through faith in him we may approach God with freedom and confidence" (Ephesians 3:12). Paul describes the source of this faith in his prayer for the hearts of the Christians in Ephesus: "I pray that out of his glorious riches he may strengthen you with power through his Spirit in your inner being, so that Christ may dwell in your hearts through faith" (vv. 16–17).

This is assurance in God because we know Him and know His heart. It isn't limited to what He can or should do for us but is grounded in who He is. It holds tight to the attributes of His faithfulness and goodness to us personally, even though we can't see Him and don't understand why He allows certain things to happen. Oswald Chambers explains, "Faith is unbreakable confidence in the personality of God, not in His power. There are some things over which we may lose faith if we have confidence in God's power only. There is so much that looks like the mighty power of God that is not. We must have confidence in God over and above everything He may do, and stand in confidence that His character is unsullied."[6] This kind of faith will get us through anything and is only made possible in relationship with Him. It's a gift from Him (2:8), faith in *Someone* more than something. That's why Paul prays for Christ to dwell in our hearts.

Keeping Your Head

The next piece of armor for prayer is "the helmet of salvation" (Ephesians 6:17). In another place, Paul describes "the hope of salvation" as a "helmet" (1 Thessalonians 5:8). Jesus is our hope in all things. We can take confidence in the salvation He won for us, understanding that nothing will separate us from God's love for us in Him—"neither death nor life, neither angels nor demons, neither the present nor the future, nor any powers, neither height nor depth, nor anything else in all creation" (Romans 8:38–39). Jesus's saving work was finished at the cross and is freely offered to us. This is more than just the hope of heaven someday; it's love that meets us today, love that rescued us the instant we repented of (turned from) our sins and trusted Him to save us.

We can't add to what He has done for us; we can only run to Him and believe.

> We can pray knowing that no matter what Satan sends our way, our Savior will see us through.

This confidence is indispensable for our prayers, and it "will be richly rewarded" (Hebrews 10:35). We can rest in it and rely on it because of its perfect and unfailing Source: "Christ in you, the hope of glory" (Colossians 1:27). He's got us, and because He does, we can pray knowing that no matter what Satan sends our way, our Savior will see us through.

When I was writing my book *Prayers for Prodigals* and our family was enduring a challenging season, God gave me a mental picture of numerous black arrows that had been sent in our direction, an aggressive spiritual attack from the evil one. But then I saw those same arrows taken and pounded at an anvil, transformed and reforged into thousands of gleaming silver arrows filling the sky, fired back at the enemy's camp. Those arrows were the prayers of God's people, who are saved and set apart for His purposes, interceding for prodigals of their own. I have seen those "silver arrow prayers" become a reality as God's people, saved and set apart, have prayed for their children with faith. Such prayer is only possible because of the Savior who has won for us "so great a salvation" (Hebrews 2:3). And that's the beauty of it—we are able to pray in more powerful ways than we imagine because of all that He is and all that He has done.

The Sword of God's Word

The sixth part of the armor for prayer is "the sword of the Spirit, which is the word of God" (Ephesians 6:17). Each piece of the armor of God, intended to help us while we pray, is itself applied to our lives *through* prayer. This is especially true when it comes to wielding "the sword of the Spirit." Instead of functioning with merely human strength, the weapons we fight with "have divine power to demolish strongholds" (2 Corinthians 10:4). Paul defines these strongholds as "arguments and every pretension that sets itself up against the knowledge of God" (v. 5). These may occur in our own thoughts and minds as well as in the lives of those around us, and this is where the power of God to move through our prayers combined with His Word must never be underestimated.

Only God can change a heart. We've probably all had the experience of trying to get through to someone, using every reason or means of persuasion at our disposal, yet we still end up getting nowhere. It's the Spirit of God who must do the work. It's the Holy Spirit who moves through God's Word and in our hearts to convict us of our sin and help us see our need for Him, calling us to salvation.

Praying the Word of God over the needs in our lives and over those we love helps us walk "in step with the Spirit" (Galatians 5:25). As we saw in the previous chapter, peace comes as we place ourselves under the Word of God when we pray, humbling our hearts before Him and trusting

Him to be faithful. God's Word goes deeper than we can fathom. The Word of God is "sharper than the sharpest two-edged sword, cutting between soul and spirit, between joint and marrow. It exposes our innermost thoughts and desires" (Hebrews 4:12 NLT). This is one of the reasons why when we pray for change in others, we often find God working on us, even bringing Scripture to mind that convicts us of our own need to change and grow.

When the devil tempted Jesus in the wilderness, Jesus quoted Scripture each time (Matthew 4:4, 7, 10). This underscores the importance of learning strategic verses for those areas where we personally need to take our stand against the enemy. When anxiety or anger or lust or envy or any other temptation threatens to lure us away from Jesus's peace, proactively searching out verses beforehand and learning them well enough to pray them the instant we are tempted can help us maintain a position of strength.

As we learn how to use the sword of the Spirit wisely, we can make progress in areas where we have struggled with the enemy's discouragement for years. We also have God's promise that as we ask for wisdom, "it will be given" (James 1:5). Paul's advice to Timothy is also on point for us: "Do your best to present yourself to God as one approved, a worker who does not need to be ashamed and who correctly handles the word of truth" (2 Timothy 2:15).

Even in our battles "when the day of evil comes" (Ephesians 6:13), there's peace to be found as we give ourselves to God in His Word and dwell there when we pray. Every day of our lives as we pray, we can be assured that God will help us. Even when we falter, His strength surrounds us and protects us. "By his divine power, God has given us everything we need for living a godly life. We have received

Fighting for Peace

all of this by coming to know him" (2 Peter 1:3 NLT). His love draws us closer still. "He is a shield for all those who take refuge in him" (Psalm 18:30 ESV).

PURSUING PEACE

- Think of a time in your life when God brought you through a spiritual attack. Thank Him for it, and then read 2 Timothy 4:18 aloud: "The Lord will rescue me from every evil attack and will bring me safely to his heavenly kingdom. To him be glory for ever and ever. Amen."
- Is there someone who has wronged you who you need to forgive? Talk to Jesus about this, and thank Him for forgiving you. Ask Him to fill your heart with His forgiveness and peace.
- Go through the armor of God in Ephesians 6 piece by piece, and ask God to apply it to your life, peace by peace.

CHAPTER NINE

Pressing through to Peace

Passionate, Persevering Prayer

*Come, you disconsolate, where'er you languish;
come to the mercy seat, fervently kneel.
Here bring your wounded hearts, here tell your anguish;
earth has no sorrows that heaven cannot heal.*

Thomas Moore

I had never chased an ambulance before, but my daughter was in it, and she was severely injured. She had just been in a multicar wreck; she and my young grandson were both in the SUV when it rolled. He emerged unscathed, but Stefani's femur was shattered, and there was trauma to her liver and internal bleeding. I happened to be in town because of a speaking engagement in the area and learned about the wreck from a kind onlooker who called on her phone for her. I pulled up as the ambulance was leaving and stayed as close as I safely could, wending my way through traffic as the sirens cleared a path.

After an agonizing wait, we were finally able to see each other in the ER as she awaited surgery. I sat by her bed, stroking her forehead and praying. My independent and beautiful daughter, in her late twenties at the time, was suddenly my little girl again, and she was hurting. We talked about how quickly the accident happened and the pain she was in, and then things were quiet for several minutes as she clasped my hand. Her quavering voice broke the silence: "Dad, I'm worried about my liver. The numbers are way high, and the doctor is recommending surgery. Dad," she pleaded, "would you please pray for me?"

I didn't hesitate. I gently placed my hand on her tummy and bowed my head, praying for the healing that God alone could bring. I can't say I prayed with anything that felt like faith; I was just a worried dad, numbed by the hard reality of my daughter's situation, doing my best to comfort her. I wanted to believe God would intervene, but there had been so many times when I prayed for healing and it hadn't happened. As I prayed, I felt like I had to wrestle with the gravity of the circumstances and my own unbelief that my prayers would make any difference. So I mustered what little faith I had and asked.

No sooner had I finished than she was whisked away for more testing and another scan of her liver. I waited there and continued to pray. Forty-five minutes later Stefani was wheeled back into the room. "Dad," she said with a relieved smile, "after we prayed, the numbers for my liver changed significantly. There's still a laceration, but it's better already, and the surgeon believes it will heal on its own and only wants to keep an eye on it for now. I really believe that God did a miracle."

That moment was a beam of bright light on what was

otherwise a dark and difficult day. God was there; He hadn't forgotten us, in spite of the trauma and my struggle to believe my prayers would make a difference. The road ahead was painful and foreboding, but we weren't alone. Stefani healed well and never required surgery for her liver.

Our family had encountered God's unexpected mercy on roads like this before, like the time our son was in rehab, detoxing from opiates, and he demanded his car keys so he could leave. The nurse, at risk to her job, refused to give them to him. Legally, he had checked himself in and was allowed to check himself out. But she had dealt with many addicts in her years and knew his life was at stake. That night Cari and I felt a need to pray hard, and God intervened in spite of the pain and mess.

But what if He hadn't? What if the very things we prayed wouldn't happen did happen? Would we still have been able to encounter His peace even in the most difficult places? Job seemed to go there when, out of the depths of his pain and despair over the loss of his health and his loved ones and possessions, he still managed to choke out the words, "Though he slay me, I will hope in him" (Job 13:15 ESV). He still had a reason to look forward and trust.

I am in awe of that kind of faith and God's ability to bring us through the unthinkable and have us emerge with our relationship with Him not only intact but somehow even more resilient. This is the depth of the love that He welcomes us into. This is the broad heart of the One who cried out from the cross, "My God, my God, why have you forsaken me?" (Psalm 22:1; Mark 15:34), expressing His agony while at the same time praying the first verse of a psalm that ends with the words, "They will proclaim his righteousness, declaring to a people yet unborn: He has done it!" (Psalm 22:31). Such are the unfathomable ways of the Ancient of Days, the eternal One who is sovereign over our conception and death and everything in between, who Himself became so human that He dared to ask "Why?" Yet He was also entirely God, able to overcome completely and declare triumphantly, "It is finished" (John 19:30).

He alone knows how to bring us through the difficult places as we cry out to Him.

Prayer That Wrestles

Prayer in our desperate moments may sound anything but holy. It grasps for words. It clings to whatever faith it can find and asks boldly. And somewhere in the grappling, it meets God, who has been there all along. We may not realize He is near; still, when we wrestle in prayer, pouring out our hearts and wills before Him, God often gives us more of His peace in ways that seem to defy our circumstances. His peace, as we have seen, is inseparable from His presence.

Prayer that wrestles to overcome our unbelief and grapples to understand what God is currently allowing in our lives is also prayer that God treasures. This isn't prayer that insists on its own way, but it may sometimes honestly include words like, "God, I thought you were my friend." It's deeper prayer, not because of any eloquence but because of its rawness. Surprisingly, prayer like this is found throughout the Bible. Think of David's words,

> O LORD, how long will you forget me?
> Forever?
> How long will you look the other way?

> How long must I struggle with anguish in
> my soul,
> with sorrow in my heart every day?
> (Psalm 13:1–2 NLT)

Or consider Jeremiah's plaintive cry, "O LORD, you misled me, and I allowed myself to be misled" (Jeremiah 20:7 NLT). We also don't want to miss Jesus's specific teaching on prayer in the parable of the man who wakes up a friend at midnight to ask for bread. Because of his "shameless audacity" (Luke 11:8), the man receives what he's asking for. And then there's the parable of the unjust judge in Luke 18:1–8, where the woman finally receives what she's asking for not because the judge is good but, in his words, "because this widow keeps bothering me" (v. 5). Scripture likewise shows us the example of Epaphras, about whom Paul told the believers in Colossae, "he is always wrestling in prayer for you" (Colossians 4:12).

> **God has placed persevering prayer in His Word for a reason, to show us not only that we can pray this way but also that He *wants us to*.**

God has placed persevering prayer in His Word for a reason, to show us not only that we can pray this way but also that He *wants us to*. Jesus's point in His parables about prayer is that because our Father in heaven is good and a friend unlike any other, we should pray with both hope and passionate persistence. There's more to this than just questioning. When we press hard in prayer, God often opens the door to meeting Him and knowing Him in ways we never have before. Genuine faith will get its hands dirty and deal with the painful and uncomfortable realities of life. It's brutally "honest to God" about our sinful brokenness and our need for a Savior. And when that honesty pours over into our prayers, they become more powerful than we know, because they touch the heart of a compassionate God who is *so* holy that He's also down-to-earth. It is God's abounding love and mercy for our helplessness that caused Him to come and live with us and die for us so that we might be with Him eternally.

"God gives where he finds empty hands," Augustine is credited with saying.[1] When we're open with Him about our depth of need, He gives us more of Himself. When our plans and ideas about how life should be have been upended and we come to the end of our self-sufficiency, He is waiting. As John Flavel wrote, "Man's extremity is God's opportunity."[2]

Previous generations had a name for this kind of prayer. They called it "importunate praying." Merriam-Webster defines *importunate* as "troublesomely urgent: overly persistent in request or demand."[3] Importunate praying keeps on pressing; it doesn't give up or take no for an answer, at least not at first. It's prayer for what we believe God would have us ask for: good things that are in keeping with who we know Him to be, wrongs and injustices that need to be righted, situations in our lives and those of others that need our Savior's touch.

Importunate prayer calls out from situations where we are powerless unless God intervenes. This is where our wills interact with God's will, not demanding our way but making our case before Him. This kind of praying is energetic, thoughtful, and passionate, as John Newton wrote:

> Come, my soul, thy suit prepare,
> Jesus loves to answer prayer;
> He himself has bid thee pray,
> Therefore will not say thee nay.
>
> Thou art coming to a King,
> Large petitions with thee bring:
> For his grace and power are such,
> None can ever ask too much.[4]

By preparing our "suit," we come before Him with reasons why we believe He should answer us, including His own Word and promises. This is prayer that engages God, pushing back against our circumstances because He's the only One who can do something about them. It is the plaintive cry that rises until either the situation changes or God gives us new peace in it.

Wrestling to Peace

In a sermon on importunate praying, Charles Spurgeon compared the way we sometimes pray with children playing "ding-dong ditch": "Too many prayers are like boys' runaway knocks, given, and then the giver is away before the door can be opened."[5] Often we need to pray more than once about something, and sometimes many more times, not because God is unwilling to listen—He listens more deeply and intently than we could possibly know—but because much more is at stake. P. T. Forsyth helps us see why this kind of praying matters so much:

> Lose the importunity of prayer, . . . lose the real conflict of will and will, lose the habit

of wrestling and the hope of prevailing with God, make it mere walking with God in friendly talk, and precious as it is, yet you tend to lose the reality of prayer at last. In principle you make it mere conversation instead of the soul's great action. You lose the food of character, the renewal of will. You may have beautiful prayers—but as ineffectual as beauty so often is, and as fleeting.[6]

Praying with importunity may not seem peaceful because of the energy involved in it. It requires that we make an effort, giving ourselves to God and praying with passion. But the result of this kind of praying is both peace and strength. Think of Paul when he asked God to remove the "thorn in [his] flesh": "Three times I pleaded with the Lord to take it away from me. But he said to me, 'My grace is sufficient for you, for my power is made perfect in weakness'" (2 Corinthians 12:7–9). Paul started in a place of begging God to take his pain away, but after he encountered God in his asking and interacted with Him, Paul ended up embracing his situation and being at peace with it, facing it with greater grace than he had ever known before.

Paul didn't receive what he was asking for, in the sense that he remained in pain. But what he received in the end caused him to "boast all the more gladly" about his weakness, "so that the power of Christ may rest upon [him]"

> **Through our praying and pleading with God, we end up drawing closer to Jesus, and the encounter with Him meets our deepest need.**

(v. 9 ESV). Paul's response shows that through our praying and pleading with God, we end up drawing closer to Jesus, and the encounter with Him meets our deepest need.

The Bible is filled with this kind of praying, and what's fascinating is that frequently the people who are pushing hard ultimately receive what they are asking for. Scripture shows us several instances of prayer that seemed to change God's mind. We may rightly push back against that, because the Bible also clearly tells us that God "is not human, so he does not change his mind" (Numbers 23:19 NLT). While that is true, if we think it through a little, we can understand that God often works with our prayers in ways that appear to be a no at first because He wants us to persevere in the asking.

An example of this is found in the pleas of the Canaanite woman whose daughter was tormented by demons. Jesus's initial response to her when she comes to Him for help is to not "answer a word" (Matthew 15:23). Her asking is so bold that it gets on the disciples' nerves. They even tell Jesus, "Send her away, for she keeps crying out after us" (v. 23). And if their lack of compassion isn't enough, Jesus's first words to her seem to push her away as well: "I was sent only to the lost sheep of Israel" (v. 24).

I believe Jesus said those words with a hint of irony, testing her faith while also calling out the prejudices of the disciples against non-Jews. What else could explain a response like that when you consider that her daughter was oppressed by demons! There must have been something about the way He said it, because she doesn't give up. The next thing she does is kneel before Him: "Lord, help me!" she cries out (v. 25). Then comes what seems like another rejection: "It is not right to take the children's bread and toss it to the dogs" (v. 26). Again and again it looks like she is rebuffed, but each time she keeps coming back. This time she responds with the words, "Yes it is, Lord. . . . Even the dogs eat the crumbs that fall from their master's table" (v. 27). Finally she hears the words she longs for: "Woman, you have great faith! Your request is granted" (v. 28). Immediately her daughter is healed and set free.

What would've happened if she had simply given up after Jesus's silence? Or after He appeared to say no the first time, or even the second? She kept making her case before Jesus, and because she did, she received what she asked for. Jesus intended to help her all along, but as with so many things God does, Jesus was operating on several levels. Think of it as three-dimensional chess from a spiritual perspective. His intent was to heal her daughter, but He also wanted her to persevere in her asking so the disciples could see her exemplary faith, overcome their prejudice, and realize that God was calling non-Jews to Himself as well. This is part of a theme that we see in other parts of Matthew's gospel. The only other time Jesus complimented someone's faith to the disciples was in Matthew 8:10, when He said about the Roman centurion, "Truly I tell you, I have not found anyone in Israel with such great faith."

Often when we're praying about one thing, God is doing another, but what He's up to will only be revealed as we keep pressing on with our prayers.

Laying Hold of God's Willingness

This mother's insistence and Jesus's ultimate answer serve as vital reminders of how much our persistent prayers matter. If we don't pray or give up praying because an answer seems unlikely, we could miss the very thing God longs to do for us. Think of God's word to King Hezekiah when he called out to Him about the Assyrian invasion outside Jerusalem's gates: "*Because you prayed* . . . the LORD has spoken" (Isaiah 37:21–22 NLT, emphasis added). There's a profound and precious truth here that's only discovered through prayer. Thus Richard Trench wrote that prayer is not "an overcoming of God's reluctance" but instead "a laying hold of his highest willingness."[7]

Other scriptural examples of wrestling in prayer include Abraham bargaining with God as he's praying for a righteous remnant in Sodom and Gomorrah. He respectfully starts by asking God if He will spare the cities if fifty righteous people remain, then forty-five, then forty, all the way down to ten. But notice how vehemently he engages God on the nature of His character: "Far be it from you to do such a thing, to put the righteous to death with the wicked. . . . Far be that from you! Shall not the Judge of all the earth do what is just?" (Genesis 18:25 ESV).

Moses prays in a similar way when God seems to want to destroy Israel with a plague in the wilderness: "What will the Egyptians think when they hear about it?" The Lord appears to change His mind when He responds, "I will pardon them as you have requested" (Numbers 14:13, 20 NLT). Notice that it's the request that makes all the difference, though God certainly knew what Moses was going to ask before he even thought of the words. Or think about Elijah, who after his showdown with the prophets of Baal goes to the top of Mount Carmel to ask for rain. He "bowed low to the ground and prayed with his face between his knees" (1 Kings 18:42 NLT). Again and again he sends his servant out to look for rain. Each time Elijah continues to pray, asking seven times until finally a cloud appears. But God had already promised Elijah that He was going to send rain (v. 1). Why was it necessary to keep on asking?

The simple answer is that Elijah knew God wanted him to. He not only knew God's character and what He'd promised, but he also clearly understood how much persevering in prayer matters to God. But Elijah was one of the greatest prophets who ever lived, able to hear and convey God's truth like few people in history. What if you or I don't have a specific promise from God about our circumstances or what we're praying for? How can we be sure that we're praying according to His will and not insisting willfully on what *we* want? This is all the more difficult if we're asking for something good, like the healing of a life-threatening illness for a child or protection for someone we love who's in harm's way. When our feelings go deep about something, it's hard for us to sort them out and discern where God is leading. How can we know how to pray when we feel overwhelmed emotionally and uncertain about God's will?

Pressing On with Hope

When my sister was seven years old, my father was in the armed services on active combat duty and was declared missing in action. Before he had shipped out for duty, he'd ordered flowers in advance for her birthday. It was now months later, and other officers had already come to our home to inform Mom that Dad was missing. Grief and worry hung heavy in the air. Then came my sister's birthday; the flowers arrived on time, neatly arranged in a small pixie vase. That was all my sister needed to see. "I know that Daddy's coming home," she reassured Mom, "because he sent me flowers." She may have had the simple faith of a child, but in the end, she was right. Dad *did* come home, and decades later she still keeps the little vase as a reminder to have childlike faith and always hold on to hope.

Of course ours is a world where daddies or mommies don't always come home, and sometimes the very thing we're praying won't happen does happen. But because my sister was able to hang on to the truth that her father loved her and was thinking about her—even though she didn't have a firm grasp of all the details—her relationship with him ultimately helped her get through the challenging season.

To pray with hope and faith, our hearts must camp out in that place of relationship with our heavenly Father. If we only see what we're praying about as a transaction of requests and answers, we may put that before our relationship with God and make our love for Him contingent upon what we're asking for. We may not mean to do this, but as we're caught up in difficult circumstances, it can easily happen. We must keep our relationship with God as our first priority so our hearts are in that place where we know we are loved by our Father and His Spirit affirms "that we are God's children" (Romans 8:16 NLT). Then we will be not only better able to pray with faith that asks boldly but also more likely to accept all outcomes. This still enables us to pray with faith, because our faith is in God and not solely in what we're asking for.

Jesus provides the ultimate example for praying like this. He carried out His life with one intent above all: leaving heaven and coming to earth for the purpose of being "the Lamb of God, who takes away the sin of the world" (John 1:29). This meant that He would voluntarily give up His life to save us from our sins. For three years He tried to help His followers understand this, but it wasn't until after His death that they saw it clearly. The night that He prayed in the garden of Gethsemane, Jesus, under incredible stress, made a breathtaking request: "Going a little farther, he fell with his face to the ground and prayed, 'My Father, if it is possible, may this cup be taken from me'" (Matthew 26:39).

We know how Jesus finished that prayer, but let's not go there too quickly. The scope of His request requires that we stop and think about what He's asking. The salvation of all who would come to Him hung in the balance. It's a stunning prayer, all the more because Jesus was the one who prayed it. His words show us the depth of His suffering and His humanness, but they also show us the breadth of what He was able to ask. Jesus did nothing outside the will of the Father, so even *His asking* on that occasion was within God's will. Imagine that! The Father allowed Jesus to ask for a way out, a change in the plan of salvation that was set "before the foundation of the world" (Ephesians 1:4 ESV). Jesus was able to wrestle in prayer with the highest possible stakes, and did so entirely without sin. Perhaps God even willed Jesus to pray that way so we could know we can pour out everything before Him when we pray as well.

Jesus finished His prayer that night—a prayer He prayed more than once—with the words, "Yet not as I will, but as you will" (Matthew 26:39). Those words underscore the truth yet again that relationship with God is everything. This is Jesus's ultimate example for us in prayer. Because everything we have is a gift from God, everything we ask for is best understood and worked out in the context of loving God and following Him.

There are times when this is anything but easy. Sometimes what God allows to happen seems to conflict with the idea that He loves us deeply or is even there at all. There are no easy answers in such moments. How could there be? There are mysteries here and things that are simply too hard to receive. If Jesus Himself were to stand in front of us and give us the reason why our child was allowed to die, would it be possible to accept it without pushing back and asking if there couldn't be another way? Life on earth has its iron finalities, but God is greater still, "though the earth give way and the mountains fall into the heart of the sea" (Psalm 46:2). Just as Jesus wept at His friend Lazarus's tomb, His heart grieves with us in our sadness and loss. And through His empty tomb He provides the ultimate hope that "earth has no sorrows that heaven cannot heal."[8]

Prayer that pushes—importunate prayer that God loves and welcomes us into—can best be understood in the context of pressing on in our relationship with Him. What will we miss if we don't? There are things that will only happen if we engage God on our deepest levels when we pray, giving Him our all. When God's sovereign will isn't immediately apparent, it's in the push and press of asking boldly that we break through to a fresh understanding of a deeper relationship with Him.

> **When God's sovereign will isn't immediately apparent, it's in the push and press of asking boldly that we break through to a fresh understanding of a deeper relationship with Him.**

A clear biblical example of this relationship-transforming outcome is found in Jacob's prayer when he was fearing the worst from his brother, Esau. God allowed Jacob to wrestle with Him until daybreak. "I will not let you go unless you bless me," Jacob told Him (Genesis 32:26 NLT). Jacob didn't only come away from that encounter with a limp. He gave the place where this happened the name Peniel, which means "face of God," because his relationship with God was forever changed. "For I have seen God face to face," he said (v. 30 ESV).

P. T. Forsyth offers an inspiring description of what God does when we engage Him wholeheartedly in our praying:

> Resist God, in the sense of rejecting God, and you will not be able to resist any evil. But resist God in the sense of closing with God, cling to Him with your strength, not your weakness only, with your active and not only your passive faith, and He will give you strength. Cast yourself into His arms not to be caressed but to wrestle with Him. He loves that holy war. He may be too many for you, and lift you from your feet. But it will be to lift you from earth, and set you in the heavenly places which are theirs who fight the good fight and lay hold of God as their eternal life.[9]

Persevering in prayer isn't just about praying harder. It's about pressing into love and, when all is said and done, finding a place to rest.

Before we leave this topic of engaging God with all that we are, we should briefly consider the helpfulness of fasting. Fasting is sometimes misunderstood as a means of gaining leverage with God by showing Him that we're really serious when we pray. Fasting has many purposes, including repentance (as David did in 2 Samuel 12:16), humbling ourselves and seeking direction from God (Nehemiah 1:4–11), expressing grief (2 Samuel 1:12), or finding strength against temptation (Matthew 4:1–11). But each of these approaches has something in common: they communicate a desire for God, for His closeness and goodness in our broken and hurting world.

Fasting isn't a way of demanding what we want from God or persuading Him to do our will. Fasting may best be understood as a yearning for God and His way more than anything else; that's why Jesus said about His followers that "the time will come when the bridegroom will be taken from them; then they will fast" (Matthew 9:15). Rightly understood, fasting isn't about what we give up—whether it's food or sex (1 Corinthians 7:5) or social media or anything else. It's actually about what we're already receiving and long for even more of: God's loving presence in our lives. Fasting is a way of focusing on God and actively placing Him above all, as Jesus did when He indicated that His "food" was "to do the will of him who sent me and to finish his work" (John 4:34). God often uses fasting to help us hear Him better and to give us new clarity and a fresh desire to serve Him—and even more of His peace.[10]

Peace Greater Than Understanding

My friend Dave Branon is a gifted writer and editor who went through an unspeakable grief. His beloved daughter Melissa was killed suddenly in a car wreck when she was seventeen years old on the last day of high school. Dave and his wife and children were devastated by her loss. His outstanding book *Beyond the Valley* recounts the struggles that followed, the pushing back in prayer and cries from the heart that only a grieving parent knows.

When I began writing this book, I asked Dave to pray for me. He pulled me aside one evening and assured me that he would, and he also gave me a Scripture passage to think about as I pondered the topic of peace through prayer. "The main reason we can find peace when we pray," he said, "is because the Lord is near." He was referring to Philippians 4:5–7, verses we considered in chapter 1: "The Lord is near. Do not be anxious about anything, but in every situation, by prayer and petition, with thanksgiving, present your requests to God. And the peace of God, which transcends all understanding, will guard your hearts and your minds in Christ Jesus."

As Dave shared this insight with me, my eyes caught a glimpse of a small ring on his finger. I immediately realized what it was. In his book, Dave writes candidly about it, a quiet thought that speaks volumes:

> Next to my wedding ring, on the little finger of my left hand, rests a girl's high school class ring. It's my daughter Melissa's.
>
> Soon after Mell died, I was in her bedroom when I found the ring. I recalled having seen it on her beautiful hand.
>
> I slipped it on and was surprised that it fit. Now I wear it all the time. Here's why: I can look at it or touch it and feel close to my precious daughter. Knowing that it graced her finger warms my heart when I miss her the most.
>
> But there's another reason I wear her ring. I want people to notice it and ask me about it. Then I can tell them of Melissa and her

life of love, faith, and fun. I hope it opens conversations that will allow me to introduce people to Melissa's Savior, and mine.[11]

True, my friend Dave had no choice but to accept the outcome of his daughter's death. But as he persisted in prayer in the days that followed, crying out to God, he found the comfort and solace that God alone can give.

Pressing through to peace is never easy. It is prayer that costs us something, laying bare the deepest desires and motives of our hearts. But our Savior meets us there, and He understands that kind of praying unlike any other. We are called to follow Him, and His path leads through Gethsemane. But we don't go it alone. There is no better Friend than He.

PURSUING PEACE

- Read Psalm 13:1–3. Thank God for the many examples of honest and persevering prayer in Scripture, and ask Him to help you be completely open with Him when you pray.
- Where in your life have you been waiting on God for an answer to prayer? Ask Him to help you be aware of His presence with you, so that you not only wait for Him but also wait *with* Him, in His peace.
- Has God allowed something in your life that you don't understand? Talk with Him about this, and ask Him to fill you with His peace.

CHAPTER TEN

The Friend Who Is Peace Forever

Prayer doesn't consist of thinking a great deal, but of loving a great deal.

Teresa of Ávila

He stood on the corner clutching newspapers for sale and cutting quite a figure with a full red beard and a horned Viking helmet. Jimmy was a member of our church with a story to tell. He had been homeless and struggled with alcohol abuse, but Jesus set him free from his addiction. Life had been hard for Jimmy. Rejected by his military dad who left his mother for another woman, Jimmy watched his mom die of cancer when he was in his teens, and his only brother, whom he lived with, died in his arms after his own battle with the disease in his thirties. On his own, Jimmy did the best he could, despite a cognitive disability.

I first met Jimmy in his forties when Ken, an elder at our church, brought him to worship. "It's nice to see you, Jimmy," I offered. "It's nice to be seen," he quipped. Ken had known Jimmy for years and frequently shared Jesus's love with him, helping him out financially and meeting with him weekly.

During those days, Jimmy had a dark side that he tried to self-medicate through alcohol and marijuana, but his panic attacks and anxiety only increased. Sometimes he spoke of hearing voices that were telling him to take his own life—"What do you have to live for?" they repeated over and over. We tried to be there for him and support him in practical ways, including helping him seek any medical or professional assistance.

It was after eight o'clock on a weekday night when Jimmy called my mobile phone while Ken and I were at a church leadership meeting. Jimmy had had too much to drink, and the voices were back. "I don't want to live anymore," he said, "and I'm afraid I'm going to do something. Please hurry."

It was a warm night and Jimmy met us in the front yard of his home. He could barely stand, but there was nowhere to sit. He put one arm on Ken's shoulder and another on mine to steady himself. Another friend from church showed up, and we made a circle. As Jimmy slurred out his worries and we did our best to listen, it was evident darkness had gained a foothold in his heart and mind. We affirmed that we cared about him and did what we could to point him to "the light of the world" (John 8:12). I encouraged Jimmy with Scripture's promise that "everyone who calls on the name of the Lord will be saved" (Romans 10:13). About an hour later he prayed with me, asking Jesus to help him out of the darkness and save him from his sins. Then we hung out with him a little longer before he went back inside.

Ken sometimes told me afterward that given Jimmy's condition that night, he was amazed our prayer together made any difference. But Jimmy *was* changed. He never drank again after that night. He also began to live with new purpose and direction. Every Sunday found him seated in the second row at church on the right, one seat over from the aisle. Jimmy still had personal struggles to face, but that night Jesus set him free from the darkness of his past, and the voices he once heard never returned. He discovered a peace he never had before, began to enjoy reading his Bible, and stood up every year around the anniversary of his sobriety to thank God during worship.

Eight years later, Jimmy succumbed to a sudden onset of a rare form of leukemia. But Jimmy had "hope as an anchor for the soul, firm and secure" (Hebrews 6:19), and looked forward to being alive in God's loving presence forever. That hope transformed his life and was the result of Jesus's presence in him: "Christ in you, the hope of glory" (Colossians 1:27). Simply put, Jimmy loved Jesus.

> **Jesus came to be our friend.**

Peace, Love, and a Friend

Jesus came to be our friend. He came to be known and loved by us and to save us from our sins and ourselves. But if you're like me, on any given day you may encounter multiple things that seem to place His peace out of reach for us. Yet that tendency exposes our difficulty; we put so much emphasis on our own efforts instead of celebrating the One who so clearly promised His peace to us (John 14:27). Either Jesus meant it or He didn't. And the purpose and passion of His life and ministry indicate He clearly did.

Can it really be that simple, that Jesus's peace is available to us every day as a gift, and all we have to do is go to Him to receive it as a gift from a friend? The refreshing answer is yes! This relationship that Jesus so longs for us to enter into and live in daily is the reason He came. John Eldredge explains,

> God is spoken of as a mystery so high and lifted up we cannot possibly be friends. The talk may be very intellectual and philosophical; it may be hyperspiritual talk of the heavens; it might be existential "dark night of the soul" stuff. Do you ever hear Jesus talk like this? Of course there are mysteries to God, but Jesus came to make God *known*. He wants to be known. He is known, by millions. This talk of distance and unknowing ushers in a great fog shrouding the way of those who *do* want to know him. It is harmful, not helpful.[1]

Even as you read those words, you may find yourself pushing back, thinking of that one instance, that terrible circumstance that happened in someone's life (or your own), that places the idea of a loving God out of reach. Or your mind goes to the brutality of the world we live in, to the apparent randomness of criminal violence and car wrecks and "nature red in tooth and claw," as Alfred Tennyson so vividly put it.[2] But ask yourself, What is my heart doing in this moment? It's not looking for an explanation as much as it's looking for hope and love. It's not seeking a reason as much as it's seeking a refuge. And that's exactly who Jesus is and what He came to be.

My mother was part of a generation that loved musicals, and because she loved to sing, now and then when I was in college she would glance at me with wide eyes and break out into a hymn she thought I needed to hear. One of her favorites was,

> What a friend we have in Jesus,
> All our sins and griefs to bear!
> What a privilege to carry
> Everything to God in prayer!
> O what peace we often forfeit,
> O what needless pain we bear,
> All because we do not carry
> Everything to God in prayer![3]

As soon as she'd start in, I'd cringe (philosophy undergrad that I was) and respond with a raised eyebrow and something like, "Life isn't a musical! It's not that simple, Mom." But there was much I didn't know or wasn't ready to accept.

Years later I learned about the life behind that hymn. The words it contained weren't platitudes; they were spiritual truth formed under the pressures of profound heartache. The author, Joseph Scriven, lost his fiancée the night before their wedding. He was there when her body was pulled from the lake she drowned in. Overcome with grief, he left his native Ireland and immigrated to Canada. He wrote the hymn as a poem in a letter to his mother, who was going through a crisis of her own.[4] Even in his profound pain, as he prayed, Scriven found in Jesus a friend who gave him comfort, hope, and peace. He made the discovery that Jesus not only took our sins on Himself at the cross; He also "took up our pain and bore our suffering" (Isaiah 53:4). And because He did, we don't have to carry it alone. He wants to help us.

Not Just Servants but Friends

Jesus made an intriguing reference to Himself in Matthew 11:19. He was repeating something the religious professionals said about Him that He was "a friend of tax collectors and sinners." The fact that Matthew, a former tax collector, remembered that and wrote it down shouldn't be missed. You have to wonder about the look on Jesus's face when He said it, if He glanced in Matthew's direction with a smile. Jesus had a heart for both tax collectors (who were seen as collaborators with Israel's Roman oppressors) *and* their polar opposites, militant Zealots (like His other disciple Simon) who sought to overthrow Roman rule by force. Somehow, because of Jesus's friendship, Matthew and Simon were able to live together in peace.

Friendship with Jesus is everything. It transforms our hearts and the way we see ourselves and others. When we come to understand prayer as an indispensable, daily part of our friendship with Jesus, it opens up new possibilities for the ways we spend time with God and for our closeness to Him. This is so much more than God being our buddy or copilot. If the idea of Jesus being our friend sounds naive or sentimental because of the way it's been misused, it helps to remember that it's also Jesus's way of describing our relationship with Him. "Greater love has no one than this: to lay down one's life for one's friends. You are my friends if you do what I command. I no longer call you servants, because a servant does not know his master's business. Instead, I have called you friends, for everything that I learned from my Father I have made known to you" (John 15:13–15).

Our life with Jesus is fulfilled in this relationship of friendship. We aren't meant to be just servants; we're meant to be closer, companions and confidants. Obedience is a vital part of what characterizes our friendship as an expression of genuine love for Him, but it isn't what initially made us His friends. He chose to love us even when we were far from Him. His loving initiative draws us close, and obedience (which He inspires and encourages through His Spirit at work within us) helps us stay near Him.

Prayer and obedience go hand in hand. When Jeremiah lamented to God, "You have covered yourself with a cloud so that no prayer can get through" (Lamentations 3:44), it was because His people had continually, willfully sinned and turned away from God and suffered the consequences on a national scale (vv. 39–42). Disobedience grieves "the Holy Spirit of God" (Ephesians 4:30). Even though the Spirit remains at work within us to convict us and help us turn from our sins, when we intentionally continue in them, we too suffer the consequences. There's a loss of both tenderness and our ability to sense God's love and nearness. But God's desire is always to soften our "heart of stone" and to help us respond with a sensitive heart, "a heart of flesh" (Ezekiel 36:26).

Jesus always wants to be our friend. And if we look afresh at prayer through the lens of friendship, it encourages us to draw closer to Him and walk into the peace that a loving awareness of His presence brings.

Friends Enjoy Each Other's Company

Regardless of where you look in history, whenever God's people try to describe what it's like to be close to Him, you find tender language. Whether it's Bernard of Clairvaux's "Jesus, Thou Joy of Loving Hearts" or Johann Franck's "Jesu, Meine Freude" ("Jesus, My Joy") or lyrics that came centuries later, like "Sweet Hour of Prayer" or "'Tis So Sweet to Trust in Jesus," there's a sense of delight that comes through. This is because God's goodness never changes, and our hearts can't help being drawn to Him.

One night many years ago when I was trying to spend more time talking to God throughout the day, I dreamt that I was in His presence all night long. Except it was more than a dream. Words fail me to describe it, but it was the happiest night of my life. I felt like I was in the presence of love and light and goodness personified, and even though I was aware of this throughout the night, I awakened refreshed, as if I'd slept soundly all night long. A couple of decades later when I was buried in books for doctoral studies, I was sitting in bed reading an account by the wife of the Puritan genius Jonathan Edwards, when I practically shouted, "There it is!" "There *what* is?" my own wife, Cari, asked, startled. "There *He* is!" I responded. "You've got to hear this, something that happened to Sarah Edwards. This is the same thing that happened to me!" I read her some of Sarah's words:

> That night, which was Thursday night, Jan. 28, was the sweetest night I ever had in my life. I never before, for so long a time together, enjoyed so much of the light, and rest, and sweetness of heaven in my soul, but without the least agitation of body the whole time. The great part of the night I lay awake, sometimes asleep, and sometimes between sleeping and waking. But all night I continued in a constant, clear, and lively sense of the heavenly sweetness of Christ's

excellent and transcendent love, of his nearness to me, and of my dearness to him; with an inexpressibly sweet calmness of soul in an entire rest in him.[5]

I know, I know. Faith shouldn't be dependent on our experiences. But it shouldn't be devoid of them either. Our loving heavenly Father, in His infinite goodness, has ways of drawing close to us that are personal for every one of His children, but His character shines through each one. Whatever century we live in, Jesus is still the same.

Friends enjoy each other's company. And when we come to see our praying as a way of enjoying God, it sets us free to spend more time with Him that way. Another Puritan writer, Matthew Henry, wrote that to live life prayerfully "is to live a life of delight in God." He describes delight as "love at rest" and asks, "Do we love to love God?"[6]

> **Friends enjoy each other's company. And when we come to see our praying as a way of enjoying God, it sets us free to spend more time with Him that way.**

It's a great question. When we learn to look forward to praying not as something we *have* to do but as something we *get* to do—an opportunity we want to participate in because we get to be with Jesus—praise, thanks, and worship follow naturally from the heart.

Friends Confide in Each Other and Share Their Interests

Jesus reminded His followers that the difference between a friend and a servant is that one knows the other's business and the other doesn't (John 15:15). David wrote in Psalm 25, "The friendship of the LORD is for those who fear him" (v. 14 ESV). The word *fear* in the Hebrew isn't limited to the negative connotations that our English word communicates. It also points to positive things like loving respect, obedience, and awe, which is why Isaiah could prophesy about Jesus that He would "delight in the fear of the LORD" (Isaiah 11:3). The combination of the words *fear* and *friendship* in the same sentence is fascinating. The Hebrew noun here for *friendship* literally means "secret" and is translated that way in several other passages. The New International Version captures David's intent by turning the noun into a verb in English: "The LORD confides in those who fear him." The meaning is the same: like a king with a friend, sometimes God lets us in on something we wouldn't know if we weren't staying close to Him in prayer.

> **Just as the closest friends can communicate with each other without words, God has ways of increasing our faith when we spend time with Him in prayer.**

We sometimes shy away from this thought because of the way we've seen it abused or misapplied, usually with the words, "The Lord told me to tell *you* . . ." But where there are counterfeits, there's also the real thing. In a previous chapter I mentioned how Cari and I felt prompted to pray hard for our son one night when he was in danger of leaving rehab early and losing his life to addiction, and there have been many other days and nights when either of our children was suddenly put on our hearts. Countless believers have stories of moments when they were immediately prompted to pray for someone and didn't know why, only to discover later the timing of their prayers was crucial.

Just as the closest friends can communicate with each other without words, God has ways of increasing our faith when we spend time with Him in prayer, even revealing to us the things we should ask for. As C. S. Lewis wrote, "It is the prophet's, the apostle's, the missionary's, the healer's prayer that is made with this confidence and finds the confidence justified by the event. . . . The fellow-worker, the companion or (dare we say?) the colleague of God is so united with Him at certain moments that something of the divine foreknowledge enters his mind. Hence his faith is the 'evidence'—that is, the evidentness, the obviousness—of things not seen."[7]

Whenever or however God lets us in on what He is doing, it's hardly ever just about us. He calls us beyond ourselves to serve Him in the needs of others. This is why the most effective efforts for God's kingdom begin and continue through dependent prayer. Friendship with Jesus through prayer helps us pull out of self-focus and instead identify with our Father's interests and align ourselves with His heart for those around us, empowering us to love and serve Him by serving them. We begin to share His burden and vision, feeling the needs around us more deeply. That's why Paul wrote to the Christians in Corinth, "For Christ's love compels us. . . . And he died for all, that those who live should no longer live for themselves but for him who died for them and was raised again" (2 Corinthians 5:14–15).

Friends Look Forward to Being Together

Years ago, Mother Teresa was interviewed by *Time* magazine about her ministry to the poor and dying in Calcutta.

When asked what she did that morning, she gave a one-word response: "Pray." When the reporter wanted to know what she did after that, she answered, "We try to pray through our work by doing it with Jesus, for Jesus, to Jesus." When asked if others should love Jesus too, her response was, "Naturally, if they want peace, if they want joy, let them find Jesus."[8]

Living for Him leads us to a growing understanding that we cannot live *without* Him. Think of Peter's words when Jesus began to challenge His followers more, and several turned back. He asked the Twelve, "You do not want to leave too, do you?" And Peter answered, "Lord, to whom shall we go? You have the words of eternal life" (John 6:67–68). The more we're with Him in prayer, the more we understand that we can't have peace without Him. Sometimes when you hear people talk about heaven, they say something like, "I'll get to see Grandma," or "Just imagine streets of gold!" Attractive as those thoughts may be, they pale in comparison to what it means to actually see Jesus and know His love perfectly.

At the end of the last book of C. S. Lewis's classic Chronicles of Narnia, Aslan the Lion (and Christ figure) turns to Peter and Edmund and Lucy and says, "You do not yet look so happy as I mean you to be."[9] A sense of anticipation hangs in the air as the children are afraid of being sent back from Narnia to the everyday world they were growing up in. But soon they discover they're staying, and their hearts fill with hope. Lewis concludes the series with the words:

> And for us this is the end of all the stories, and we can most truly say that they all lived

happily ever after. But for them it was only the beginning of the real story. All their life in this world and all their adventures in Narnia had only been the cover and the title page: now at last they were beginning Chapter One of the Great Story which no one on earth has read: which goes on forever: in which every chapter is better than before.[10]

Lewis is pointing to the kingdom of God that has entered into our world and will one day arrive with finality, the "new heavens and a new earth" God promises to all who love Him, where creation will be restored and "the wolf and the lamb will feed together, and the lion will eat straw like the ox" (Isaiah 65:17, 25). God will personally live with His people, and "he will wipe every tear from their eyes, and there will be no more death or sorrow or crying or pain. All these things are gone forever" (Revelation 21:4 NLT). At last we'll be where we were always meant to be, and words alone fail to describe the joy of it.

But in the meantime, we're not there yet. Jesus is with us through His Spirit, but we also long for more, because there's no peace like the peace He gives. Even here our Savior and Friend lifts our eyes to something more, and He is at the heart of it. "There is no relief like prayer," Charles Spurgeon wrote. "All you want between here and heaven is stored up in Christ Jesus."[11]

Helmut Thielicke was a pastor and theologian who suffered persecution for his stalwart witness to Christ and the Word of God under the Third Reich. Toward the end of World War II, he was faithfully serving a congregation in Stuttgart as the country was in ruins. He recalls,

My work in Stuttgart seemed to have gone to pieces; and my listeners were scattered to the four winds; the churches lay in rubble and ashes. On one occasion when I was absorbed in these gloomy thoughts I was looking down into the concrete pit of a cellar which had been shattered by a bomb and in which more than fifty young persons had been killed. A woman came up to me. . . . Then she said, "My husband died down there. . . . All that was left was his cap. We were there the last time you preached in the cathedral church. And here before this pit I want to thank you for preparing him for eternity."

In that moment he realized, "All of a sudden God had opened a door to his kingdom, in the moment of catastrophe and in the midst of the collapse of the personal worlds of two persons. There it was between that woman and myself."[12] Even in the worst of circumstances, Jesus gives us comfort and hope as we look to Him and as His Spirit lifts our eyes to the unconquerable good that is on the way and even now is breaking in.

This broken world will assail our peace, but it cannot take it from us, because it's not of this world. Our peace is the gift of the One who holds all things, who will one day make the world entirely new. And *we* will get to see it and live in it. Best of all, we will get to see *Him* and live with Him. He is the One who loves us like no other, who calls us His friends and laid down His life so that we may have His and live in the beauty of His presence forever.

Until then, He has given us prayer as His way to respond

to His love and receive the gift of His peace. As we turn to Him in our hearts, we are changed by His Spirit and daily discover our home with Him. He welcomes us to step out of the world's frenzied pace, to "come away" (Mark 6:31 NASB) and lean into Him so we might humbly share our every care with Him and be refreshed by His peace. He speaks incomparable truth to us through His Word and strengthens us for the long journey, helping us to look forward to the day that is dawning.

Through prayer the door to His kingdom opens even here, and the light streams in: "goodness and peace and joy in the Holy Spirit" (Romans 14:17 NLT). As we walk in that light, we do not walk alone. The One who loves us more than life is there with us, and He will never fail.

PURSUING PEACE

- Read John 15:13–15, and thank Jesus for being your Savior, Friend, and Peace.
- Ask Him to help you to be a friend to Him and to walk closely with Him through obedience.
- Read Jude 24–25, and praise God that He wants you to live and discover more of His peace and joy forever.

Acknowledgments

Writing a book is a little like going on a journey to a new but distant place. It starts with a sense of adventure and with careful planning. Along the way there are friends and companions who offer wisdom and encouragement through all the ups and downs. The difference between writing books and going on long journeys is that once you arrive at your destination (and the book is complete), there's no long trek home. Because finishing a book feels like arriving at a longed-for destination and coming home at the same time, I offer a depth of gratitude for each of those who shared the journey and made the adventure a trip worth taking.

There have been many. Cari, your love and commitment expressed in the most practical things cannot be overstated; I love you. Noemi, Stefani, Geoffrey, Sarah, Austin, and Leilani, your companionship along the way is always a joy. To the team at Our Daily Bread Ministries, it's the privilege of a lifetime to work with you. Dawn Anderson, Sarah De Mey, Chriscynethia Floyd, Paul Brinkerhoff, and Dave Branon, you have been outstanding for your skill, patience, faith, and encouragement. Joel Armstrong, your patience and gifted insights while editing this manuscript have been an answer to prayer. Lisa Samra and Amy Boucher Pye, your kind help is a blessing. The prayers of the faithful at Peace Church and your kind understanding for your pastor have been a gift from start to finish. Ken Davis, Jan Gray, Bob and Pam Dodson, Rick and Julie Soles, Lynn Wiemann, Jim and Jill Hanson, Mark and Skip Honeck, Bev Campbell, Dennis Carrey, Dr. Larry and Pat Howell, Derrick and Joy McMillan, Tim and Heather Kidd, Craig and Paula Shaw, a simple thank-you is not enough—I owe you a debt of prayer. The Coastal Mid-Atlantic prayer group, you have been an exemplary source of inspiration more times than I can count. John Holecek, Phil Thrash, David Beaty, and Don and Dy-Anne Long, your stalwart prayers have been a consistent and powerful help.

"To the only God our Savior be glory, majesty, power and authority, through Jesus Christ our Lord, before all ages, now and forevermore! Amen" (Jude 25).

Notes

Chapter One: Heart First

1. John Maynard Keynes, "Economic Possibilities for Our Grandchildren," Yale Department of Economics, accessed June 8, 2023, http://www.econ.yale.edu/smith/econ116a/keynes1.pdf.
2. John Calvin, *Institutes of the Christian Religion*, I.11.8.
3. Alexander Allen, *Phillips Brooks: Memories of His Life with Extracts from His Letters and Notebooks* (New York: E. P. Dutton and Company, 1907), 605–6.
4. Henri J. M. Nouwen, *The Path of Peace* (New York: Crossroad, 1995), 23–24.
5. Andrew A. Bonar, *Heavenly Springs: Portions for the Sabbaths of a Year* (Edinburgh: Banner of Truth Trust, 1986), 87.
6. C. S. Lewis, *Mere Christianity* (Westwood, NJ: Barbour and Company, 1952), 167–68.

Chapter Two: Peace with Our Past

1. John Newton, *Letters by the Rev. John Newton*, ed. Josiah Bull (London: Religious Tract Society, 1869), 218.
2. George Herbert, "Conscience," Christian Classics Ethereal Library, accessed June 30, 2023, https://www.ccel.org/h/herbert/temple/Conscience.html. First published 1633 in *The Temple*.

Chapter Three: Peace We Were Meant For

1. Rosalind Rinker, *Prayer: Conversing with God* (Grand Rapids, MI: Zondervan, 1959), 23.
2. Dallas Willard, *The Spirit of the Disciplines: Understanding How God Changes Lives* (San Francisco: HarperCollins, 1991), 263.
3. Augustine, *Confessions* 1.1.1.

4. C. S. Lewis, *Mere Christianity* (Westwood, NJ: Barbour and Company, 1952), 173.
5. George MacDonald, *George MacDonald: An Anthology*, ed. C. S. Lewis (New York: Macmillan, 1947), 42.
6. Martin Luther, as quoted in Billy Graham, *Peace with God, The Secret of Happiness, Answers to Life's Problems: His Greatest Works* (New York: Inspirational Press, 1995), 47.
7. G. K. Chesterton, *Orthodoxy* (Garden City, NY: Doubleday and Company, 1959), 160.
8. See my book *Praying the Prayers of the Bible* (Grand Rapids, MI: Our Daily Bread Publishing, 2018).
9. G. K. Chesterton, *The Collected Works of G. K. Chesterton*, ed. Aidan Mackey, vol. 10, *Collected Poetry: Part 1* (San Francisco: Ignatius Press, 1994), 43.

Chapter Four: Peace in Our Worries

1. Oswald Chambers, *Prayer: A Holy Occupation* (Grand Rapids, MI: Discovery House Publishers, 1992), 22.
2. For more on our family's struggle with addiction and how God helped Geoff overcome it, please read the book we cowrote together, *Hope Lies Ahead: Encouragement for Parents of Prodigals from a Family That's Been There* (Grand Rapids, MI: Our Daily Bread Publishing, 2020).
3. Helmut Thielicke, *Faith: The Great Adventure* (Philadelphia: Fortress Press, 1985), 34.
4. William Cowper and John Newton, *Olney Hymns* (London: Whittingham and Arliss, 1815), 199.
5. P. T. Forsyth, *The Soul of Prayer* (Gearhart, OR: Watchmaker Publishing, 2012), 67. First published 1916.
6. Bernard of Clairvaux, "Jesus Thou Joy of Loving Hearts," Hymnary, accessed July 5, 2023, https://hymnary.org/text/jesus_thou_joy_of_loving_hearts.

Chapter Five: Peace and Rest

1. This phrase comes from *The Practice of the Presence of God* by the seventeenth-century friar Brother Lawrence.
2. Robert J. Morgan, *Then Sings My Soul: 150 of the World's Greatest Hymn Stories* (Nashville: Thomas Nelson, 2003), 199.

Chapter Six: Peace in Low Places

1. C. S. Lewis, *The Screwtape Letters* (New York: HarperCollins, 2001), 69–70. First published 1942.

Notes

2. C. S. Lewis, *Mere Christianity* (Westwood, NJ: Barbour and Company, 1952), 153.
3. Paul E. Miller, *A Praying Life: Connecting with God in a Distracting World* (Colorado Springs, CO: NavPress, 2009), 125–26.
4. Charles Haddon Spurgeon, *Beside Still Waters: Words of Comfort for the Soul*, ed. Roy H. Clarke (Nashville: Thomas Nelson, 1999), 3.
5. John Piper, "Charles Spurgeon: Preaching through Adversity," Desiring God, January 31, 1995, https://www.desiringgod.org/messages/charles-spurgeon-preaching-through-adversity.
6. Charles Haddon Spurgeon, "The Minister's Fainting Fits," *Lectures to My Students, The C. H. Spurgeon Collection* vol. 1 (Rio, WI: Ages Software, Inc., 1998–2001), 176.
7. Spurgeon, "The Minister's Fainting Fits," 177.
8. Charles Haddon Spurgeon, "Joy, Joy for Ever," The Spurgeon Center, accessed October 20, 2023, https://www.spurgeon.org/resource-library/sermons/joy-joy-for-ever/#flipbook/.
9. Charles Haddon Spurgeon, "Zion's Prosperity," *The C. H. Spurgeon Collection* vol. 44 (Rio, WI: Ages Software, Inc., 1998–2001), 395.
10. Charles Haddon Spurgeon, "Ejaculatory Prayer," *The C. H. Spurgeon Collection* vol. 23 (Rio, WI: Ages Software, Inc., 1998–2001), 893.
11. Charles Haddon Spurgeon, "The Preacher's Private Prayer," *Lectures to My Students, The C. H. Spurgeon Collection* vol. 1 (Rio, WI: Ages Software, Inc., 1998–2001), 49.
12. Philip Yancey, *Prayer: Does It Make Any Difference?* (Grand Rapids, MI: Zondervan, 2006), 191.
13. Spurgeon, "Ejaculatory Prayer," 899–900.
14. Spurgeon, "Ejaculatory Prayer," 900.
15. Spurgeon, "Ejaculatory Prayer," 901.
16. Spurgeon, "Ejaculatory Prayer," 902.
17. Arthur Bennet, ed., *The Valley of Vision: A Collection of Puritan Prayers and Devotions* (Edinburgh: Banner of Truth Trust, 1975), xxiv.

Chapter Seven: Hungering for Peace

1. "The Westminster Larger Catechism," Evangelical Presbyterian Church, accessed October 20, 2023, https://epc.org/wp-content/uploads/Files/1-Who-We-Are/B-About-The-EPC/LargerCatechismModernEnglishORIGINAL.pdf.

2. Dietrich Bonhoeffer, *Life Together* (New York: Harper and Row, 1954), 84.
3. Dietrich Bonhoeffer, *Psalms: The Prayer Book of the Bible* (Minneapolis, MN: Augsburg Fortress, 1970), 9–12. Interestingly, after Bonhoeffer wrote this book, the National Socialist German government under Hitler forbade his ever publishing in Germany again.
4. David Beaty, *An All-Surpassing Fellowship: Learning from Robert Murray M'Cheyne's Communion with God* (Grand Rapids, MI: Reformation Heritage Books, 2014), 69.
5. Daniel Henderson, *Fresh Encounters: Experiencing Transformation through United Worship-Based Prayer* (Colorado Springs, CO: NavPress, 2004), 85.
6. Robert Murray M'Cheyne, *A Basket of Fragments: Notes for Revival* (Geanies House, UK: Christian Focus, 2019), 190.
7. For a more comprehensive collection of Scripture's prayers, please see my book *Praying the Prayers of the Bible* (Grand Rapids, MI: Our Daily Bread Publishing, 2018).

Chapter Eight: Fighting for Peace

1. Charles Haddon Spurgeon, *Morning and Evening: Daily Readings*, Evening, November 3, Christian Classics Ethereal Library, accessed July 7, 2023, https://ccel.org/ccel/spurgeon/morneve/morneve.d1103pm.html.
2. William Cowper and John Newton, *Olney Hymns* (London: Whittingham and Arliss, 1815), 156.
3. Oswald Chambers, *So I Send You and Workmen of God* (Grand Rapids, MI: Discovery House Publishers, 1993), 115.
4. Andrew A. Bonar, *Heavenly Springs: Portions for the Sabbaths of a Year* (Edinburgh: Banner of Truth Trust, 1986), 107.
5. Corrie ten Boom, *The Hiding Place* (New York: Bantam, 1974), 238.
6. Oswald Chambers, *If You Will Ask: Reflections on the Power of Prayer*, updated language edition (Grand Rapids, MI: Discovery House Publishers, 2012), 44–45.

Chapter Nine: Pressing through to Peace

1. Augustine of Hippo, as quoted in C. S. Lewis, *Letters to an American Lady* (Grand Rapids, MI: Eerdmans, 2014), 73. First published 1966.
2. John Flavel, *Keeping the Heart: A Puritan's View of*

Maintaining Your Relationship with God (Geanies House, UK: Christian Focus, 1999), 95.
3. *Merriam-Webster*, s.v. "importunate," accessed July 10, 2023, https://www.merriam-webster.com/dictionary/importunate.
4. William Cowper and John Newton, *Olney Hymns* (London: Whittingham and Arliss, 1815), 25.
5. Charles Haddon Spurgeon, "The Importunate Widow," *The C.H. Spurgeon Collection* vol. 15 (Rio, WI: Ages Software, Inc., 1998–2001), 130.
6. P. T. Forsyth, *The Soul of Prayer* (Gearhart, OR: Watchmaker Publishing, 2012), 94.
7. Richard Chenevix Trench, *Notes on the Parables of Our Lord* (London: John W. Parker, 1841), 291.
8. Thomas Moore, "Come Ye Disconsolate, Where'er Ye Languish," Hymnary, accessed July 11, 2023, https://hymnary.org/text/come_ye_disconsolate_whereer_ye_languish.
9. Forsyth, *The Soul of Prayer*, 94–95.
10. For more information on how to fast, please consider "Prayer and Fasting," lesson 7 of my "Prayer Basics" course on Our Daily Bread University: https://odbu.org/lessons/sf120-07/. It may be helpful to consult with a medical professional before fasting from food, especially if you are diabetic or have had an eating disorder.
11. Dave Branon, *Beyond the Valley: Finding Hope in Life's Losses*, 10th anniversary ed. (Grand Rapids, MI: Our Daily Bread Publishing, 2020), 181.

Chapter Ten: The Friend Who Is Peace Forever

1. John Eldredge, *Beautiful Outlaw: Experiencing the Playful, Disruptive, Extravagant Personality of Jesus* (New York: FaithWords, 2011), 174–75.
2. Alfred Tennyson, "In Memoriam A.H.H.," 1850.
3. Joseph Medlicott Scriven, "What a Friend We Have in Jesus," Hymnary, accessed October 10, 2023, https://hymnary.org/text/what_a_friend_we_have_in_jesus_all_our_s.
4. Robert J. Morgan, *Then Sings My Soul: 150 of the World's Greatest Hymn Stories* (Nashville: Thomas Nelson, 2003), 131.
5. Jonathan Edwards, *The Works of Jonathan Edwards*, ed. Edward Hickman, vol. 1. (Peabody, MA: Hendrickson Publishers, 1998), cvii. First published 1830.
6. Matthew Henry, *A Method for Prayer* (Geanies House, UK: Christian Heritage, 2009), 221–22. First published 1710.

7. C. S. Lewis, *Letters to Malcolm: Chiefly on Prayer* (New York: Harcourt Brace Jovanovich Publishers, 1964), 60–61.
8. Edward W. Desmond, "Interview with Mother Teresa: A Pencil in the Hand of God," *Time*, December 4, 1989, https://content.time.com/time/subscriber/article/0,33009,959149,00.html.
9. C. S. Lewis, *The Last Battle* (New York: Collier Books, 1980), 183.
10. Lewis, *The Last Battle*, 184.
11. Charles Haddon Spurgeon, *Beside Still Waters: Words of Comfort for the Soul*, ed. Roy H. Clarke (Nashville: Thomas Nelson, 1999), 210.
12. Helmut Thielicke, *Our Heavenly Father: Sermons on the Lord's Prayer* (New York: Harper and Brothers, 1960), 65–66.

Spread the Word by Doing One Thing.

- Give a copy of this book as a gift.
- Share the QR code link via your social media.
- Write a review of this book on your blog, favorite bookseller's website, or at ODB.org/store.
- Recommend this book to your church, small group, or book club.

Connect with us. f ⓞ

Our Daily Bread Publishing
PO Box 3566, Grand Rapids, MI 49501, USA
Email: books@odb.org

Love God. Love Others.

with Our Daily Bread.

Your gift changes lives.

Connect with us.
Our Daily Bread Publishing
PO Box 3566, Grand Rapids, MI 49501, USA
Email: books@odb.org

"Come and talk with me."
—Psalm 27:8

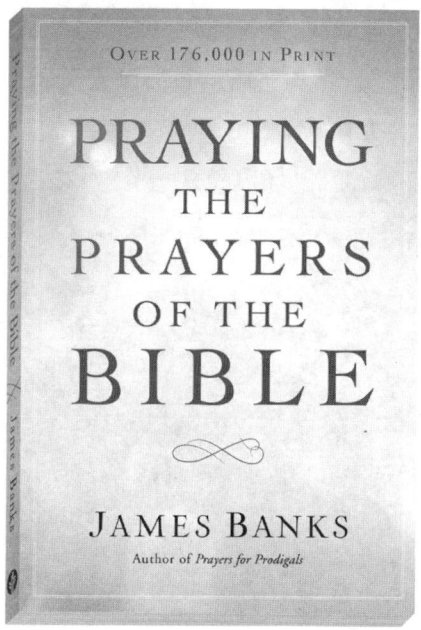

Worship the Lord and petition Him for your needs with this powerful collection of scriptural prayers taken straight from God's Word.

Get Yours Today!

No child is too far to reach.

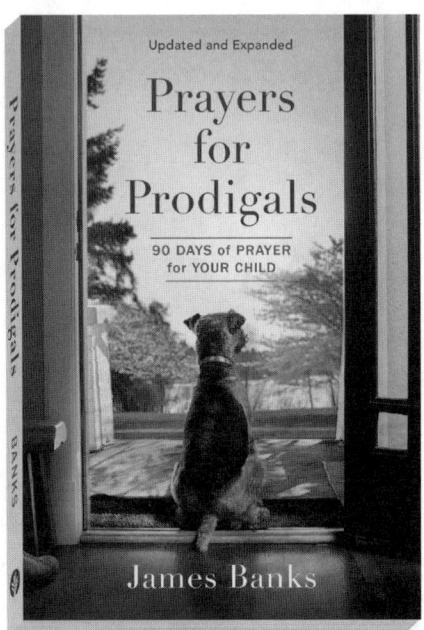

When you're the parent of a prodigal, you know you can never pray enough. *Prayers for Prodigals* offers daily prayer helps and group study questions for families to support one another. As you face heartbreak and hopelessness, this book points to the ultimate source of hope—God. It will encourage you and your family to trust Him.

Get your copy today!

No prodigal is beyond the reach of God.

James Banks and his son, Geoff, each tell their own side of the story through Geoff's prodigal journey, a journey that ends in redemption and hope.

Buy It Today!

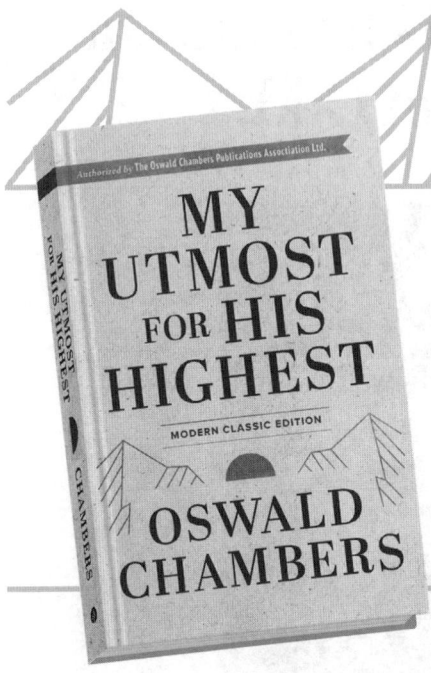

A Modern Classic to Inspire Your Faith

The timeless wisdom of Oswald Chambers shines in this new Modern Classic Edition of the beloved 365-day devotional first published by his widow in 1927. With a thoughtful approach to the language and context of the original, the author's voice has been carefully preserved and the Bible texts updated to the New International Version. Full of powerful challenges to devote your all for God's highest glory, these readings open the way to deeper, stronger faith.

Buy It Today